"It's been 10 years since Daniel was our National Account Manager, but I still remember him fondly. He was client-centric and results-focused. If you want to **create value for your clients and improve sales results**, then I recommend you read *STEP UP!*"

—Dale Brown, Manager, **Dow Chemical**

"We've had Daniel speak to our sales teams twice. Why? *STEP UP!* provides easy-to-understand and easy-to-execute **advice for improving sales performance and business results**. I recommend you step up and get this book!"

—Lee Butcher, Workplace Diversity Officer, **Medtronic**

"Daniel provides the insight, inspiration and tools to help you get off your assets and step up to the next level. **If you're serious about personal development, you've got to read this book!**"

—Desi WIlliamson, **Hall of Fame Speaker/Author**

"*STEP UP* is a great combination of inspiration and practical steps to improving your performance and creating greater business success. **This book will help you get on track and stay on track.**"

— John Kremer, *1001 Ways to Market Your Books*

"This book does a great job of taking the science and research on motivation, goal setting, and accountability, and putting it into an inspirational and practical package. **I have no doubt that those who follow Daniel's wisdom will step up in their careers!**"

—Don Conlon, Chairperson, Department of Management
Michigan State University

Step Up!

DANIEL GRISSOM

*"Daniel is a unique blend of business thinker and
personal motivator. He helped our organization.
I recommend you read this book!"*
Tim Armstrong, President,
Advertising & Commerce, Google

Step Up!

How to
WIN MORE
and *Lose Less*
in BUSINESS!

NEW YORK

STEP UP!

How to WIN MORE and *Lose Less* in BUSINESS!

ISBN: 978-1-60037-306-0 (Hardcover)

ISBN: 978-1-60037-307-7 (Paperback)

Published by:

MORGAN · JAMES
THE ENTREPRENEURIAL PUBLISHER™

Morgan James Publishing, LLC
1225 Franklin Ave Ste 325
Garden City, NY 11530-1693
Toll Free 800-485-4943
www.MorganJamesPublishing.com

Habitat
for Humanity®
Peninsula
Building Partner

Cover and Interior Design by:
Tony Laidig
www.thecoverexpert.com
tony@thecoverexpert.com

To my mother – the late Dr. Pauline Grissom

Because the best of me comes from you.

FOREWORD

———•———

Though we had yet to meet, Daniel and I seemed to be two ships passing in the middle of the night. Not only was he knee-deep completing the requirements for his MBA degree, Daniel was looking forward to launching his corporate career. I, on the other hand, was serving on the faculty at his alma mater (The Atlanta University School of Business) and was looking forward to a much needed break and the completion of my first book: *Think and Grow Rich- A Black Choice*. As fate would have it, more then ten years later our paths crossed again and this time we connected. I was working on my fifth book: *Have vs. Have Not – What Black Millionaires Know that Others Do Not*. And Daniel was cutting his teeth with Fortune 500 powerhouses such Google, IBM, and Eli Lilly carving a niche in the training and consulting fields.

Like so many of his corporate clients, I was immediately impressed by Daniel's can-do attitude and no excuses approach to life. It was clear that here was someone driven by a deep desire to make a difference. During our brief encounter he not only shared his short and long term goals, but he placed into my hand the last self help book that anyone would ever need: *Step Up! How to WIN MORE and Lose Less in Business*. Written for those who refuse to waste a single moment in regret or living far beneath their possibilities, **this is a handbook for excellence and effectiveness.**

What would it take for you to alter the course of your life? What are the factors that separate peak performers from average men and women? What is the one quality that not only leads to success in business but life as well? If you've ever pondered these ideas and concepts as I have, or sought answers to some of life's most challenging questions–in and out of the world of work– it might be time for you to *Step Up!* And it's never too soon to start. Louder than words, this is not a book to be consumed in one or two sittings. Rather, **this is a book to be read, absorbed, and placed into practice**. Consider this to be a supplement to keep on your office desk or night stand and dip into whenever needed. As your personal "performance improvement coach," Daniel guides you every step of the way by utilizing his *Six Steps for Winning More and Losing Less in Business:*

> *Raise Your Standards*
>
> > *Identify Your Talents*
> >
> > > *Consistent Self Evaluation*
> > >
> > > > *Proper Preparation*
> > > >
> > > > > *Unleash Your Potential*
> > > > >
> > > > > > *Invest in Coaching*

Packed with personal anecdotes and written in Daniel's distinctive inspiring voice, *Step Up!* offers deep insights, original thinking, and solutions to nuts-and-bolts problems that will change the way you consider your life's work. **These tried and true keys will lead anyone–from newly minted college graduates to CEOs–to sales and career success.** Unlike so many useless and worn out "how to" tomes that crowd the marketplace today, *Step Up!* is a high energy, welcome edition that speaks to each of us no matter where we may find ourselves within the corporate hierarchy.

So what's the bottom line? Life changes only when you act on what you've learned. From this day forth **you are invited to become the master of your career**. *Will you accept the invitation?* You need only to listen to Daniel Grissom's wise counsel and *Step Up!*

Dennis Kimbro

July, 2007

ABOUT THE AUTHOR

When Daniel Grissom talks, sellers and leaders pay attention.

He works with executives at blue chip companies including Google, IBM, Eli Lilly Walgreens, NASDAQ and Mastercard. His message is global – he has spoken to sellers and leaders in Asia, Africa, Europe and the USA.

As an insider into excellence for close to two decades, Daniel has discerned what works (and doesn't work) in the achievement of superior sales results. His personal experiences and field observations lead to a discovery of six steps that make 80% of the difference in achieving superior results. These six actions are *STEP UP! – The Acronym of Excellence.*

He knows these truths because **he has been in the trenches with sellers and leaders, which is where the battle for behavior change is won and lost.** Daniel's abilities are unique in that he has the tools to accurately identify your DNA for Results and the talent to effectively unleash it. In 2005, his talents were recognized by Google when they hand-picked him as their dedicated sales training consultant.

Daniel's passion for professional development began at Michigan State University where he earned his degree in business. Thereafter, he began his career as a Congressional Liaison where he helped where he spoke with community groups and helped constituents solve problems. Never settling for less than the best, Daniel stepped up and earned his

MBA from Atlanta University. After graduation, he advanced into major account sales. For a decade, he served as a National Account Manager in the transportation industry, managing corporate giants including Dow Chemical and DaimlerChrsyler. Later, he worked with Rand McNally and Tony Robbins. In 2004, as a speaker, Daniel was voted MVP of the world's most prestigious consultative sales training organization – the Huthwaite Corporation. He is a CPBA, CPVA and CAIA, which are certifications that equip him to identify and interpret individual and organizational DNA. Recently, **Daniel was awarded an honorary Ph.D.** from Cornerstone University of Jerusalem in recognition of his out-standing contributions to the advancement of Christian Education in the USA, Africa and Asia.

Daniel is a family man, devoted to his wife Taisia and son Isaiah. Daniel created the PhD in Results Company and dedicated it to the memory of his mom, the late Dr. Pauline Grissom, who graduated with her Ph.D. from the University of Michigan in 1975.

INTRODUCTION

For close to a decade, I have led strategy sessions for business executives at Google, IBM, Eli Lilly, NASDAQ, UPS, ExxonMobil, Walgreens and Mastercard in a mission to improve individual performance and business results. These business summits combined with my upbringing and field experiences have provided the insights to develop STEP UP! It's an acronym that identifies 6 steps that make 80% of the difference in the achievement of superior results.

$$6 \text{ STEPS} = 80\% \text{ DIFFERENCE}$$

I am *Daniel West Grissom* and I named my company "PhD in Results" in my mother's honor. She was my queen and my coach. She had the heart of Oprah, the wit of Mary Tyler Moore, the wisdom of Proverbs and the occasional "backhand swing" of Serena Williams!

Her name was *Pauline West Grissom*. She was the only one of her three siblings that went to college. But my mama didn't stop at this level; she stepped up and earned her Ph.D. while working as a leader in the Detroit Public School system. She worked in the *Research & Evaluation* Department and was responsible for developing assessments and solutions to help students improve their performance and results. This was her personal passion.

Sadly, my mother died in 1994 of a brain aneurysm, but her spirit lives on through me. The "PhD" represents excellence in research and evaluation. The "Results" represents excellence in action and achievement. And privately, the "PhD" whispers that "Pauline had Daniel (PhD)," and that I am obliged to continue her mission to help others step up to the next level. Like mama, this has become my personal passion.

My *research and evaluation* regarding performance improvement began in earnest during my years as a fledgling M.B.A. and sales representative at Union Pacific Railroad. I was a good communicator and problem-solver, but I didn't know how to sell. I knew how to talk. Soon, I discovered that effective selling and leading is less about talking and more about asking and listening.

I began studying sales, leadership and excellence vigorously. I applied what I learned and, in time, my results began to step up! I advanced to CSX Transportation as a National Account Manager and then to Rand McNally as the Manager of Business Alliances. Later, I worked with Tony Robbins and Huthwaite – both are premiere training and development companies.

My professional journey from "mediocrity to mastery" has not been an easy one, as you'll find out as you read this book. I trust you'll find this hard-won wisdom helpful to you in business and the business of life.

What makes this book different form those already published? Four factors:

1. It invites you to become the CEO (Chief Excellence Officer).

Let's face it. We're living in a highly competitive market where individual performance is the difference between organizational profit and loss. This means that you must step up and **become the CEO** (Chief Excellence Officer) of the privately owned company called you. *Your mission?* It's to **win more and lose less** in business. *Your method?* It's to **achieve excellence** in all endeavors. *Your model?* **STEP UP! – The Acronym for Excellence.**

My promise and your payoff: Every idea, tip and suggestion in this book is focused on helping you improve your performance and results.

Everything you find here is the result of many years of research, interviews and personal experience. I know it works because I've watched it work for others and it's worked for me too. So, the content here is not theory.

Each of the STEP UP elements is discussed in detail with information presented in a n easy-to-follow and high visual manner.

STEP UP stands for:

Standards

Talents

Evaluations

Preparation

Unleash **P**otential

2. It inspires you to earn your PhD in Results!

In the world of education, a PhD is a degree which signifies that a leader has stepped up and committed themselves to excellence in academics. But, in the world of business, a PhD is "the degree" that a leader has stepped up and committed to excellence in action!

Simply put, a PhD in education is about being school smart, but a PhD in Results is about being street smart. You see, the schools test to determine how smart you are, but the streets test to determine how you are smart! *Get it?*

It's not about having to go back to school to get years of education to improve your results. It is about having to go inside yourself to make the small changes that can make a BIG DIFFERNCE in the improvement and achievement of superior results.

In summary, a PhD in Results is a psychology. It's a commitment to excellence, action and the achievement of superior results. *How can you earn your PhD in Results?*

Well, it's simple. You've got to STEP UP!

3. It teaches you how to uncover and unleash your DNA for Results!

Every person is born with a one of-a-kind biological DNA. DNA is your unique composition of internal factors that are responsible for the natural strengths and struggles within us. *Had you considered that you have a professional DNA, too?* You do. And it's equally as unique as your biological DNA.

Yet, most books about sales effectiveness assume that the seller possesses the natural DNA required for success in that job and that the seller is committed to changing their behavior. Regretfully, **these book-smart assumptions get mugged on the streets of reality and results don't improve**. In contrast, this book is based on an inside/out approach which recognizes that success is an inside job.

Consider this. Every year, Fortune 500 companies spend over a billion dollars on performance training with a mission to improve sales performance and results. The supposition underlying most of these investments is that mediocre performance is primarily due to the lack of effective sales skills (techniques) and strategies (positioning). Sadly, the lack of skills is rarely the primary cause of lackluster sales performance. **The root cause is often the lack of self-discipline and self-development.**

The harder (older) model that many individuals and organizations use to improve performance is to invest in skills training, then add strategies, and then leave it to the individuals to handle the "self (evaluation)" portion on their own. In short, 90% of the focus is on Skills, 10% on Strategies and basically 0% on Self. This results model uses an "outside-in" approach for improving performance. But, this is ineffectual because results begin from the "inside-out", not the "outside-in."

The Results Model

Harder Model

Results

- Self
- Strategies
- Skills

Smarter Model

Results

- Skills
- Strategies
- Self

The smarter (newer) model used by top performing individuals and organizations takes the older model and turns it inside out. They begin with the "Self" component – by identifying their DNA and ensuring that it effectively matches the requirements of the job – then they invest in performance training that unleashes their DNA for Results.

Why is this more effective? It's more effective because "knowledge of self" is the best motivator and behavior modifier in the world! Furthermore, if a seller lacks the self-discipline or mental horsepower, then even the best skills training in the world can't produce improved results. *Does that make sense?* Too often, skills training is an external solution to an inner issue. It's a prescription that treats the symptoms of sales ineffectiveness, but does not remedy its root causes.

4. It's universal!

STEP UP! is applicable to individuals and organizations. The content written in the beginning of each chapter focuses on the individual – you. The later pages in each chapter focus on the organization – your company.

STEP UP! is applicable to all lines of business, including Sales, Marketing, Customer Service, Operations, etc. That's because this is a book about achieving excellence. Moreover, STEP UP! adapts to all aspects of life including Education, Non-Profits, Family, etc. So, if you're a non-sales or non-business person reading the book, then just substitute the term "seller" and insert the name of your role. It's just that simple.

TABLE OF CONTENTS

—————

Part I

THE RESULTS CHALLENGE

Today's challenge is to produce more results with fewer employees for customers who demand more for less.

BILL BONNSTETTER
CEO, Target Training International

THE RESULTS CHALLENGE

Does this sound familiar? Your family is asking you to earn more money and spend less time at work. Your clients are demanding more value and at lower costs. Your competition is increasing while your differentiation is decreasing. And your CEO is expecting you to achieve more results this year with fewer resources. **This is the Results Challenge.**

The collision of these challenges is causing painful problems in sales and leadership. Organizations are hustling to stay alive, while individuals are struggling to stay employed.

Almost every day we see headlines like these in the Wall Street Journal, NY Times and Businessweek:

BellSouth Executives asked to leave in wake of AT&T takeover

Ford layoffs could hit 30,000

NBC cutting TV workforce – slashing 700 jobs in effort to be more nimble

Recently, I received an email entitled **"Still Got a JOB..."**. While I changed the name for anonymity, the email is real. It captures the essence of the results challenge that sellers and leaders are facing.

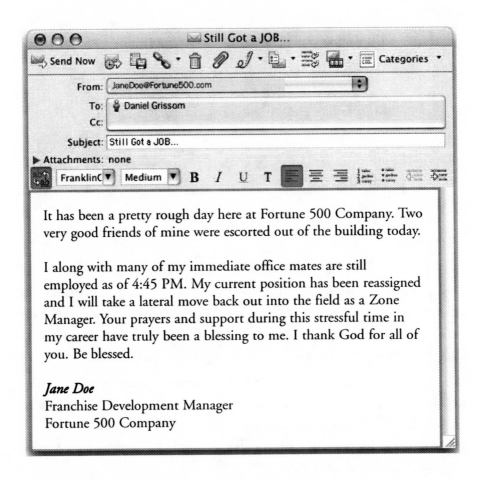

It has been a pretty rough day here at Fortune 500 Company. Two very good friends of mine were escorted out of the building today.

I along with many of my immediate office mates are still employed as of 4:45 PM. My current position has been reassigned and I will take a lateral move back out into the field as a Zone Manager. Your prayers and support during this stressful time in my career have truly been a blessing to me. I thank God for all of you. Be blessed.

Jane Doe
Franchise Development Manager
Fortune 500 Company

Here's the reality about today's fierce market, if you operate as an employee you're vulnerable. The future demands that you "manage it like you own it!" It requires that you adopt an entrepreneurial or intrapreneurial mindset. It invites you to step up and **become the CEO (Chief Excellence Officer)** of the privately owned company called you.

THE MARKET FORCES

*The future has several names. For the weak it is impossible.
For the fainthearted, it is unknown.
For the thoughtful and valiant, it is ideal.*
—Victor Hugo

We live in a rapidly changing world of increased commoditization and decreased differentiation. What was "good enough" yesterday is considered "unacceptable" today. Business success today, and in the future, is achieved by those who not only anticipate the market shifts and trends, but who are able to re-evaluate, re-focus and re-engineer themselves.

Through my work and evaluation of some of the most successful companies in the world, I have identified three key market forces that are significantly impacting individual performance and organizational results. The intersection of these challenges are **driving leaders at all levels** to rethink the way they do business and **STEP UP** to the next level. These market trends are:

1. Radical Change

2. Increased Commoditization

3. Hiring Top Talent

CHALLENGE # 1 – RADICAL CHANGE

We live in a world of rapid, relentless and radical change. Windows of opportunity open for only a brief moment, and then slam shut. The pace of innovation continues to accelerate and what was impossible yesterday is probable today. Technology raises the standard and changes the rules for results. New products, even whole markets, appear, mutate and evaporate suddenly.

Goldman, Nagel and Preiss, authors of *Agile Competitors and Virtual Organizations*, forewarn us that "rapid, relentless and uncertain change is the most unsettling marketplace reality that companies and people must cope with today."[1]

CHALLENGE # 2 – COMMODITIZATION

For both products and services, in every industry, commoditization is unceasing and unforgiving! Even the most agile individuals and organizations are struggling. While suppliers develop differentiation strategies to increase their margins, their clients develop purchasing strategies to shrink these margins and drive value to the lowest common denominator – price.

This is how Chan Kim, author of the best-selling *Blue Ocean Strategy*, traces the process of commoditization:

> *Accelerated technological advances have substantially improved industrial productivity and allowed suppliers to produce an unprecedented array of products and services. The result is that in increasing numbers of industries, supply exceeds demand. The trend toward globalization compounds the situation. As trade barriers between nations and regions are dismantled and as information on products and prices becomes instantly and globally available, niche markets and havens for monopoly continue to disappear. The result has been accelerated commoditization of products and services, increasing price wars and shrinking profit margins.* [2]

CHALLENGE # 3 – HIRING TOP TALENT

The third blockade on the road to results is talent. In particular, this challenge involves the hiring, developing and retaining of top talent. Face it, today's market conditions demand that you have the right people in the right positions doing the right things. Regretfully, most organizations do a weak job of this, which leads to turnover, competitive disadvantage and

---

1. *Agile Competitors and Virtual Organizations: Strategies for Enriching the Customer* by Steven L. Goldman, Roger N. Nagel, Kenneth Preiss

2. *Blue Ocean Strategy: How to Create Uncontested Market Space and Make Competition Irrelevant* by W. Chan Kim, Renée Mauborgne

weak results. An effective system for hiring, developing and retaining top talent is "no longer a should, it's a must!"

Consider these comments from leading authorities on this subject:

Larry Bossidy, author of *Execution*, writes:

The leaders most important job is selecting and appraising people.

Jim Collins, author of *Good to Great*, writes:

We expected that Good-to-Great leaders would start with vision and strategy. Instead, they attended to people first, strategy second. They got the right people on the bus, moved the wrong people off, ushered the right people to the right seats — and then they figured out where to drive it.[3]

THE MARKET HAS STEPPED UP, SHOULD YOU?

You have two choices: Either Step Up or get stepped on!
DANIEL GRISSOM

The facts are clear and indisputable. The market conditions have stepped up. *How does this affect you?*

It means you must work smarter, not harder. You must raise your standards, maximize your talent, make superior evaluations, prepare properly and unleash your potential.

You must constantly look for ways to improve yourself, create greater value for your clients and achieve superior sales results. You must deliver a high Solutions-to-Problems Ratio by consistently increasing solutions and decreasing problems.

---

3. *Level 5 Leadership*, Jim Collins, Harvard Business Review, July-August, 2005

Think about it, you have three options to increase results:

1. Decrease your problems
2. Increase the solutions
3. Do both!

RESULTS = SOLUTIONS - PROBLEMS

MONEY OR EXCUSES?

You can make money or excuses.
But, you can't make both at the same time!
MAMA

My analysis of top and average performers reveals that the major difference between these two groups is their mindset. Top performers hold themselves personally accountable. Top performers find a way or make a way to achieve great results. They don't make excuses.

Average performers always seem to find or make a way to "snatch defeat from the jaws of victory." It's the market's fault. It's their boss. It's the company. It's the client. There's always a reason for not delivering the desired result.

To become a top performer you absolutely must put aside those excuses and take responsibility for results. The choice is yours. **You can make money or excuses, but you can't make both at the same time.**

THE MINDSET

- It's never the market or another person.
- It's always me.
- No Excuses offered. None Accepted!

A perfect example of a top performing company is Dell. Its success is based on its famous business model and its ability to achieve at an extremely high level. High expectations and consistent execution are embedded in the company's DNA. Here's what Michael Dell said in an interview with *The Harvard Business Review*:

> *We don't tolerate businesses that don't make money. We used to hear all sorts of excuses for why a business didn't make money, but to us they all sounded like "The dog ate my homework." We just don't except that.[4]*

Good to Great author Jim Collins provides a great example of the difference between executives in top performing organizations vs. those in average organizations:

> *Steel companies Bethlehem Steel and Nucor both faced a competitive challenge from cheap imported steel. Both companies paid significantly higher wages than most of their foreign competitors. Yet executives at the two companies held completely different views of the same environment.*
>
> *Bethlehem Steel's CEO summed up the company's problems in 1983 by blaming the imports. "Our first, second, and third problems are imports." Ken Iverson and his crew at Nucor saw the imports as a blessing: "Aren't we lucky. Steel is heavy, and they have to ship it all the way across the ocean, giving us a huge advantage!"[5]*
>
> *What was the major difference between these two companies?*

The difference was mindset and a commitment to excellence. One stepped up and achieved a great result. The other fell back and provided a great reason for the lack of results.

---

4. *Execution Without Excuses*, Thomas Stewart, Harvard Business Review, March 2005
5. *Level 5 Leadership*, Jim Collins, Harvard Business Review, July-August, 2005

MODIFY OR MAGNIFY?

————•————

Your results can only grow to the extent that you do.
JIM ROHN
Business Philosopher

Today's fierce market conditions offer you two options: **Either you magnify your performance or modify your goals.** If you neglect to select the former, then the market will impose the latter on you. Either you settle for less or step up for more. It's just that simple.

THE CHOICE IS YOURS

- Either Magnify your performance or Modify your goals.
- You decide today.
- The market will test you tomorrow.
- The truth will be revealed.

The following African proverb is a great parallel for today's market conditions of "hunt or be hunted."

Every morning in Africa, a gazelle wakes up. It knows it must run faster than the fastest lion or it will be killed. Every morning a lion wakes up. It knows it must outrun the slowest gazelle or it will starve to death. It doesn't matter whether you are a lion or a gazelle. When the sun comes up, you better start running. And fast!

THE ACRONYM FOR EXCELLENCE

What's the solution to the results challenge?

The solution is for you and your team to STEP UP! It's a six-step system for improving performance and results. It's the acronym of excellence.

As an insider into excellence for close to two decades, I've been able to discern what works (and doesn't work) concerning the improvement and the achievement of superior results. These field observations led me to **the discovery of a dozen things that make 80% of the difference in achieving superior results.** STEP UP! is a simple, logical and exceedingly effective methodology created from experience inside the guts of world-class corporations in the USA, Asia, Africa and Europe.

Here's the breakdown of the STEP UP! acronym:

Standards . . . . Raise Your Standards

Talents . . . . Identify Your Talents

Evaluations . . . . Consistent Self-Evaluation

Preparation . . . . Proper Preparation

Unleash Potential . . . . Unleash Your Potential

Let's take a quick look at the key components of each step. Then, we'll explore these topics deeper:

Standards. Standards are where you set the bar for yourself. Your commitment to results. High standards produce high results. Average standards produce average results. It's just that simple.

Talents. Each of us has not only a physiological DNA, but also a professional DNA – the skills, talents and drive that make you who you are. When you understand your DNA and align it, then you'll see your results dramatically increase.

Evaluations. Evaluations are the questions you ask yourself and the decisions you make. Ask good questions and you'll make good decisions. Maintain Consistent Self-Evaluation and you'll achieve superior results.

Invest in Coaching

Unleash Your Potential

Proper Preparation

Consistent Self-Evaluation

Identify Your Talents

Raise Your Standards

Preparation. When you learn to anticipate the future and create an action plan for bridging the gap between where you are now and where you want to be, you'll see your results improve.

Unleash **P**otential. This is the action and execution portion of the model. It's great to have high standards, talents and plans, but until you actually do something with all that, you're not going to achieve results.

Coaching. If you take a look at the world's top performers across all professions, you'll find a common denominator – the best use coaches. Top performers are continuously raising the bar and the means to that end is inevitably great coaching.

Part II

THE BUSINESS SOLUTION

We are in a highly competitive marketplace where individual performance is the difference between organizational profit and loss.

BILL BROOKS
The Brooks Group

Step One

RAISE YOUR STANDARDS

Sometimes you deliver performances that are substandard.
Raise your standards. Always keep your standards at or
above what we must achieve to propel the company
forward as a global company of excellence.
RAM CHARAN
What The CEO Wants You to Know

Are your standards high enough to achieve the results that your CEO demands and Wall Street rewards?

How do you know if you possess high standards? Here's a key – look at your results. If they're not exceeding the expectations of your boss, clients or yourself, then your standards of excellence are probably questionable.

The good news is, your standards will get you the results you want. The bad news is, same thing – your standards will get you the results you want. See, the results you get are in direct proportion to your concept of excellence.

If "pretty good" represents excellence to you, then that's what you'll get. But, if you want superior results, then you must set superior standards. *Why?* Because your results are always in direct proportion to your standards.

Ironically, most people never think to define their own standards. They also neglect to recognize the standards of their partners, alliances, and team members. The result is psychological confusion and lower results. The prevailing assumption in business is that everyone on the team, including you, are equally committed to excellence. That's nonsense because each of you operates with a different unconscious definition of "excellence." The resulting mismatch creates what I call an, "excellence gap."

What is a standard? A standard is an internal goal. It's your inner drive to achieve a desired result. It's a reflection of what you consider to be acceptable or unacceptable behavior regarding results. It's your self-imposed measure of excellence. In summary, it's your personal commitment to be the best.

So, reach inside yourself and ask, *"Am I curious or serious about achieving superior sales results? Committed or just interested? Playing around or playing to win?* This gut-check is critical because superior commitment is the basis for achieving superior results in sales and leadership.

Too often, the quest to achieve extraordinary results is undermined by an ordinary commitment. Think about it. *Can a salesperson with a $50,000 standard achieve a $500,000 result? Or can an organization achieve a billion dollar result with a million dollar commitment?* Of course not! An individual or organization can never outsell or outperform their commitment to excellence.

So, let me ask you a question: *How commited are you to your own success? Is it time to set a new standard?*

Top-performers step up by demanding more and more of themselves and seek to reach their upper limit. However, average performers do not demand more of themselves because for them, "mediocre" is their upper limit. Their lower standards are self-imposed restraints on their results. So, if you're not achieving the results you desire, then its time to look at your standards.

Don't be casual about your standards because casualness leads to casualties.

> ## STANDARDS ARE:
>
> * Your self-imposed measure of excellence.
> * Your commitment to achieving a goal.
> * Your Results Philosophy

You see, everything affects everything else. Every discipline or lack of one affects every other discipline. Mistakenly, a leader says, "this is the only place where I let down." That cannot be! Every low standard will adversely affect the rest of your performance. Why? Because doing less than you are capable of doing invites mediocrity, which permeates all other standards.
JIM ROHN

PERSONAL EXCELLENCE

Your results are directly related to your philosophy, not the economy.
EARL SCHOFF

A philosophy is a way of thinking. It's a system of beliefs. It's a reflection of your standards. *What's your personal philosophy concerning results?* Think about that for a minute because your personal philosophy is a major determining factor in how your results turn out in business and life. With your permission, I'd like to share a portion of my personal story with you because it illustrates the impact your philosophy can have on results.

I grew up in Detroit, the middle child in a middle class, well-educated family. My father was a lawyer and my mother was a teacher. As mama used to say, "You weren't exactly raised by wolves."

My mother, Pauline, was the consummate STEP UP example for me. Though I didn't have a name for it at the time, my mama was world class in everything she did. As well, she embedded the STEP UP principles into me and my brothers.

She was a teacher, wife, and mother who was always stepping up. For instance, she returned to graduate school to earn her Masters degree, while working and raising three boys. Then, she earned her PhD in Education, which was followed by a scholarship to law school. These were amazing accomplishments for anyone, but particularly so for a black woman in the 1960s and 1970s.

I spent my high school years at Cass Tech in the Detroit public school system, and despite mama's high standards, I wasn't a stellar student. When I think about my results philosophy it was to "aim for an A when the class was easy or settle for a C when the class was hard." My goal was to "get by." *Have you ever been there? Still there in certain aspects of your life?*

This "just enough to get by" mentality permeated my scholastic results for many years. Sure the school systems could have been better. Sure, my teachers could have been better. But, **things would have been better for me, if I had given a better me.** *Do you get it?* Your personal results will always be congruent with your personal standards. Regretfully, many of us "aim for easy and settle for average" in sales and leadership. *What new results could you achieve in the next 12 months by raising your standards?*

The standards of a man can be observed
in the mirror of his results!
DANIEL GRISSOM

Following high school I was accepted into Michigan State, contingent upon being enrolled in a "special student" program, which required that I be tutored because of my mediocre scores and grade point average.

I graduated four years later with a business degree and pretty much the same mediocre results. Mama helped me get a job with a U.S. Congressman following college, and it was here that my standards started to rise. *What happened?*

Part of it was certainly just maturing and becoming an adult, but there was something else. I was doing something that I loved – helping people. Traditional schooling wasn't always the best fit for my DNA – but now I was beginning to identify my unique talents and unleash my potential.

There was another important change and new influence during this time period. I was working with and surrounding myself with people whose standards were significantly higher than mine. I began to refine my personal philosophy and raise my standards. You see, your results philosophy and standards are always affected by those of your peer group. In other words, **whoever you spend your time with you become.** *What affect is your peer group having on your results?*

> *It's easy to remain mediocre. All you need to do is spend major time on minor things with minor people.*
> JIM ROHN

After a couple of years working with the Congressman, I decided to STEP UP and set a new standard. I enrolled at Atlanta University to earn my MBA. This time around my results were dramatically different. I graduated with a 3.6 GPA – quite different from my 2.5 undergraduate GPA. The difference – my personal philosophy and standards!

You see, to improve your performance, **you don't need a better economy you need a better philosophy.** You don't need more skill, you need more will. *Is your current results philosophy serving or sabotaging you?*

What happened to me next? Well, I'll continue my story in the next chapter. But enough about me for now. Let's return to our broader discussion about improving your results.

THE PURPOSE OF SELLING

The purpose of a business is to create and keep a client.
PETER DRUCKER

What's the purpose of selling? Marinate on that question for a moment because your answer will reveal your personal philosophy and standards. The answer will have major implications on your behavior and results in business.

If you could write you own personal dictionary, what would you write under selling? All the actions you and your organization take will flow from this definition. It will affect your sales strategies. It will impact your sales call planning and execution. It will effect how you treat your clients.

I believe the purpose of the sales call is to help your client succeed. It's the ultimate standard of excellence. Think about it. The sales call is not about what you want to get, but what you plan to give on the call. You want to give the gift of sight and insight. **You want to help your clients to think, act and win.**

Face it. The market is saturated with sellers, but it's thirsty for solvers. *Have you adjusted your approach to quench your clients' thirst?* To do so, you must be in solve mode, not sell mode. You must be more client-centric and less seller-centric.

Notice that I used the word **client, not customer**. *What's the difference?* Well, consider this fact. The dictionary defines a client as being one that is under the protection of another or a dependent. In contrast, the word customer is defined as one that purchases a commodity or service. *So which do you really have, clients or customers? Which do you really want?*

While we're at it, let's take a look at the use of the word **solve vs. sell**. *What's the difference?* Well, consider this fact. The synonyms for sell are to unload, to hawk people or dispose of. In contrast, the synonyms for solve are to decipher, to unravel and to find a solution. Don't get me wrong – we must sell on the call. But, I have found that **when you solve well you sell well**, especially when it comes to the major sale.

So, you must raise your standards and create more value during each client interaction or dialogue. **You must bring your seeds to the call, not your needs to the call. You must help your clients to think, act and win.** This is the purpose of selling.

ACHIEVING SALES EXCELLENCE

In order to close more sales you've got to create more value
DANIEL GRISSOM

Sales Results! *What other words in business are used so much and pursued so aggressively?* It's the universal language of senior executives, sales management and sales teams. And so often, achieving results means getting the business or closing the deal. Yet **the challenge of getting the business begins with our responsibility of creating value for the client.**

Consider this: The more value you create, the more business you'll get. And of course, the opposite is true: The less value you create, the fewer sales you will get. So, let's talk value. In fact, let's first define value. *How do you define value?* In plain words, creating value is about being helpful to your clients. And the more helpful you are to them, then the more value you'll be creating for them.

Our clients are more sophisticated and better-informed. Our clients are demanding relationships that produce results. Our clients are demanding more value and less selling. *What does that mean to you?* It means you must bring your clients insights that they cannot discover on their own. It means you must provide your clients with unexpected value during each engagement. **It means you must set a new standard for the quality of your sales calls.**

Try less to become a man of success and seek more to become a man of value.
ALBERT EINSTEIN

How can you be more helpful to your clients when engaging them in a business dialogue? My experience and field research reveals that there are **three primary ways you can create value and differentiate yourself**. Here they are:

First, you can be helpful to your clients by providing them with **new ideas**. That's right, providing your clients with new ideas on how to avoid pain (business problems) or achieve gain (business goals) in their business. When you've succeeded in creating this kind of value, then you may hear your clients say, "I hadn't thought of that before" or "That's a good point", etc.

Second, you can drive more value by giving them a **better understanding** of the business challenges or opportunities that they may have underestimated. Perhaps the client has a partial handle around something, but they don't really understand its full impact. When you've succeeded in creating this kind of value, then you may hear your clients say, "I can see that more clearly now" or "Oh, now I get it".

Third, you can be helpful by giving your clients access to your **key contacts**. This is making your rolodex available to the clients by giving them access to subject matter experts, alliance partners and other specialists. When you've succeeded in creating this kind of value you may hear your clients say, "Thanks for introducing me to John" or "I'm glad you brought her into the discussion".

In summary, our mission as value creators should be to provide clients with **new ideas, better understanding and access to our rolodex because these behaviors produce results**. The fact is that you're either creating value or eroding when you're in front of a client. It's just that simple. *Are you creating value or eroding it during your sales calls? Are you creating enough value during the sales call that the client would be willing to pay for your consultation?*

RAISE YOUR GAME

Most men are anxious to improve their circumstances, but are unwilling to raise their standards. Therefore, they remain bound.
JAMES ALLEN
As a Man Thinketh

Top performing athletes, like corporate athletes and entrepreneurial tri-atheletes, set high standards for themselves and it shows in their results. Consider Tiger Woods. He became a professional golfer at age 20. He won four of the first 15 tournaments he entered, which earned him over $60,000,000 in prize money and endorsements that first year. In 1997, he won his first Masters – the PGA's most prestigious tournament. Thereafter, Woods examined the videotape of his performance and decided that his swing was not as good as it could be. He decided to raise his standards on his personal performance.

Woods committed to perfecting his swing. This required him to first re-engineer it. In doing so, his results initially took a dip for the worse. He won only one tournament over the next 19 months.

Then what happened? In early 1999, Woods mastered his new swing. He won 10 out of 14 tournaments and won six consecutively, which is unheard of in golf. Later, Woods became only the fourth player in the history of golf to win the Grand Slam, achieving these results before his 25th birthday!

What's the moral of this story?

The moral of the story is that "good" is often the enemy of "great." Think about it. Tiger was already on top of his game, but he decided to "step up" and raise his standards from "good to great!" As the graphic illustrates, you must step up to the next level in order to achieve the next level of results. Superior results aren't reserved for the super-talented. They're available to anyone who is willing to step up and get on the path to proficiency, then stay on it!

Your Standards	Your Results
Great	Great
Good	Average
Average	Poor

So, what's your golf swing?

In other words, *what's the one area of your behavior that, if mastered, could explode your results in the next 12 months?*

THE TIGER IN YOUR EYE

You've gotta bring it to get it!
MAMA

When an athlete possesses an extraordinary hunger for winning and results we say, "he's got the eye of the tiger." It's the mental and emotional edge that makes the difference between winning and losing in sales and life. *Is the tiger in your eye?*

Below are excerpts from an interview, conducted by Don McKneely of *Minority Business News*, with Tiger Woods that provides insight into this expression and "Tiger, the man."

MBN: *What is your strongest motivator?*

Tiger: Winning! I'm very competitive, and winning is everything. If I'm at my best – I'm hard to beat.

MBN: *What is your mantra or strategy for winning?*

Tiger: First of all, be in tip top shape. I work out every day, seven days a week. Exercise and an optimally healthy, controlled diet are key. Secondly, practice, practice and practice. **Practice with strategic preparation equals perfection.** This is what separates the great from the good. Additionally, mind control and concentration. Applied concentration is the difference between winning and losing. I always play to win – ALWAYS.

MBN: *With the pressures of being one of the greatest golfers of all time to ever play, how do you handle the day-to-day stress of things you deal with?*

Tiger: Focus, focus, focus. My dad taught me to pick a spot out on the green and to shoot or putt exactly to that spot. The same mindset applies to the course of life. If you pick a spot where you want to be, then focus and refocus and you will eventually hit that spot.

MBN: *What is one of the key lessons you've learned while on the world tour?*

Tiger: **It's important to change whatever you're doing wrong to improve – even if it means losing at the time.** It's all about building and growth. If you lose this round, but learn things that help you win the next three in a row, that makes you a long-term winner and that's where you want to be.

Do your current standards reflect that the tiger is in your eye?

THE PURSUIT OF EXCELLENCE

————•————

Perfection is our goal, but excellence will be tolerated.
VINCE LOMBARDI

Let's take a look at a few additional examples of individuals and organizations that have consistently raised the bar on results. Consider modeling their standards and passion of excellence.

Michael Jordan. On the basketball court, his personal standards and commitment to excellence were the basis for his superior results. Think about it. He first came to our attention with the game-winning shot in the 1982 NCAA championship game for the North Carolina Tar Heels. He entered the NBA in 1984 after being named an All-American twice and leading the 1984 U.S. Olympic team to a gold medal.

Jordan entered the NBA as the 3rd pick in the draft that year and was chosen by the Chicago Bulls, who were the league's perennial losers. As a rookie, he averaged 28 points per game. That's the result of someone who believes in raising the bar, and it was still rising. He went on to seven consecutive scoring titles, slam-dunk championships, MVP performances and finally three consecutive world championships and a starring spot on the 1992 Olympic Dream Team.

Those were his personal results, *but what about the team results?* With Jordan leading his teammates, the Bulls advanced from worst to first in a few short years. *How'd they do that?* It began with Jordan continually raising his personal standards.

In doing so, he raised the standards of his teammates. Jordan's self-driven quest for results had a multiplier effect on his performance and his teammates. It was his commitment to excellence that transformed his team and gave them six NBA championships.

Consider the comments from Jordan's coach for most his career, Phil Jackson, who said:

"The thing about Michael is he takes nothing for granted. When he first came into the league in 1984, he was primarily a penetrator. His outside shooting wasn't up to professional standards. So he put in his gym time in the off-seasons, shooting hundreds of shots each day. Eventually, he became a deadly three-point shooter."

As the corporate or entrepreneurial tri-athlete, *what aspects of your professional game should you work on?*

United States Marine Corps. Like other branches of our military, the few, the proud, the Marines take raw talent and teach young soldiers how to improve individual performance and team results. This process begins in boot camp where each individual is "invited" to step up his or her personal standards of excellence. Superior standards and results are instilled as their code of conduct. Is it any wonder that Marines compliment each other with the word, "Outstanding!"

After boot camp and advanced training, their performance improvement process accelerates as each individual is greeted with challenges that test his or her heart and commitment to the mission. Marines carefully evaluate themselves to ensure that their actual performance aligns with their potential best. The Marines' motto is *Semper Fidelis*, which is Latin for "Always Faithful." Their personal pledge is to be faithful in giving their best to the mission at hand, their fellow Marines and their families.

The following summarizes it well. It is a letter published in the *Washington Times* on September 25, 1998, by the Marine Corps co mandant at that time:

Since becoming the Marine Corps commandant more than three years ago, I have drawn the line when it comes to standards. I have not only pledged to uphold our standards, but have actually raised the bar when it comes to being a Marine - enlisted or officer.
—General C.C. Krulak, Commandant USMC[6]

---

6. *Washington Times*, September 25, 1998

But what about the business case? All that HooRah is great, but does it make dollar sense? Let's look at some data:

> *The Marine Corps provides America the best return for its military dollar, receiving about 6.5 percent of the Department of Defense budget and in return providing about 20 percent of the U.S. forces combat power. To do this and remain the nation's leading force-in-readiness, the Corps periodically re-evaluates its operational capabilities and adapts to the changing situations of the world.*
>
> —Marines Magazine, April 1, 2005[7]

How faithful are you in giving your personal best to your organization and your clients?

Lexus. Let's compare the standards of GM to Lexus. What's "good enough" for GM is unacceptable for Lexus. Lexus has the highest standards in every facet of its business from design to manufacturing to customer service. Consumers see that and respond to it.

Do a simple Google search on Lexus Standards and GM Standards. What you find are two dozen references to *The Lexus Standard*. No one has to explain it; we know what it is by virtue of the automobile manufacturer's actions and behavior. We can look at the quality of the product and services. Lexus is so synonymous with high standards that the highest standard for the industry is referred to as "The Lexus Standard."

Lexus standards are 100% in tune with the client and his or her overall experience. It's what the client perceives as important that's important to Lexus and guides its standards. With Lexus, it's not just a pretty car; it's a car that you can truly trust. I have personal friends whose Lexus cars have traveled in excess of 200,000 miles. That's the norm – not the exception!

The Lexus standard is client-centric and focuses on results. In contrast, GM seems to be more seller-centric or production- centric, focusing

---

7. *Marines Magazine*, April 2005

on activities like paint compound formulas and audit controls. GM would be the brand of choice if mass production was the success criterion, but it's not. Success is based on high quality and superior performance. With that in mind, it's easy to see why GM struggles and Lexus succeeds in being the top selling luxury brand with the most loyal clients.

What did these examples of top performing individuals and organizations have in common?

They had a passion for excellence which drove them to raise their standards. They competed with themselves and their potential, not against others. They chose to STEP UP!

In what key areas should you and your team raise the bar and set a new standard?

SEE IT. BELIEVE IT. ACHIEVE IT.

Whatever the mind can conceive and believe, it can achieve.
NAPOLEON HILL
Think and Grow Rich

Stephen Covey made famous the phrase *Begin with the end in mind.* Though certainly overused, it is an extremely powerful concept. *What does it mean for you?*

In order to produce superior results, you must first decide what superior results look like. You must create a vivid mental picture of the end results you want because the creation of all results begin in the mind. And once you imprint that vision in your mind, you will then begin to find ways to achieve it.

Your vision must be more than just a vague desire or dream. It must be specific and clear.

One of the keys to maximizing your results is based on the accurate evaluation of your standards. Sadly, most individuals and organizations neglect to evaluate their own standards. *What causes such behavior?* I believe the first factor is that most automatically conclude, without evaluation, that they already have high standards. The second reason is that standards are difficult to measure because they are not tangible or visible.

Standards for Results

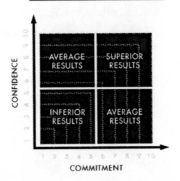

Top performers think on paper and use visuals like this one to help them create a vivid mental picture and accurately assess their standards. This enables them to be more conscious about their standards and the necessary changes to increase their standards and results.

Top performers know that high standards are the foundation for superior results. They also know that the raw material that cements this foundation is their personal commitment and confidence. In other words, their foundation is built on their desire to achieve the goal and their belief that it will be achieved.

DEFY THE ODDS. SET A NEW STANDARD.

High standards are tough to define, but easy to identify.
MAMA

Picture yourself at the top of the mountain about to launch yourself down the mountain as fast as you can in pursuit of winning the gold medal at the Winter Olympics. Your confidence drove you to step up and reach for such an ambitious goal. And your commitment ensured you'd prepare and do the necessary work to achieve it.

That's where Vince Poscente found himself. Poscente was a skier who dreamed of being a World Champion – an Olympic Gold Medalist. The problem was that Poscente was just an average skier. However, two factors converged that made his dream a potential reality. First, the Olympic Committee added a new winter sport that did not require as much training and experience as other events. Second, Poscente was committed to defying the odds, setting a new standard and stepping up!

He put little yellow dots everywhere – in his wallet, on his dashboard, on his toothbrush. The dots were a visual anchor of one thought, **"I AM A CHAMPION!"** When he began to believe it, he began to ski like it.

He began to do the work to ensure he was mentally and physically prepared to be on that mountain during the 1992 Olympics. Although Poscente didn't win a gold medal that day, he became a Speed Skiing Finalist and five-time national record holder. What matters most is that he was a winner, because he had given his personal best.

By the way, Poscente's event required him to ski in a straight line directly down the mountain. On his way down, he reached a top speed of 135 mph!

In what area of your professional life should you set a new standard, defy the odds and STEP UP?

THE ATTITUDE OF EXCELLENCE

*You must develop the ability to achieve positive results
under negative circumstances*
MAMA

I believe the first step toward exemplary results is a **No Excuses** standard of excellence. I've studied the differences between average and top performers and at the top of that list is a **No Excuses** standard of excellence. Top performers don't have excuses. Average and below average performers always seem to find someone else to blame. There's always a reason why they aren't more successful. It's the market. It's their boss. It's the company.

In order to be a top performer you absolutely must put aside those excuses and take 100% responsibility for your own results. That goes for individuals and it goes for companies.

Are you a creator of results or a creator of reasons? I love this question because it encapsulates everything I'm trying to impart in this chapter. You're either creating results or reasons, raising or lowering standards; it's just that simple.

Would you like to know something that is simple and easy to do that can dramatically change your attitude and results? I call it the *Responsibility for Results Mantra*. Repeat after me.

It's not the market.
It's not the client.
It's not my boss.
It's not the product.
It's not the company.
It's not the other person.

It's always me.
I must find a way or make a way to achieve superior results.

LEADERSHIP COMMITMENT

*Leadership is not holding another person to your standards;
that's management. Leadership is getting another person
to create extraordinary standards for themselves.*
TONY ROBBINS

Setting higher standards without holding people accountable may be worse than not setting a higher standard at all. That's because if you don't actively measure performance and hold people accountable, you are saying to them that the higher standard is not important, that it really doesn't make a difference.

If a manager is fearful of or doesn't agree with the goals set down for him by his superiors, he may set and communicate standards for his team in a way that tells them he is merely following instructions from above. He may in fact unconsciously hope that his subordinate's performance falls short, which then reinforces his belief that the goals were inappropriate to begin with.

When a manager doesn't show full commitment to standards, the results are the same as setting standards and not following up. Either way you're telling people higher standards aren't important.

There are several psychological challenges that influence the level of standards set and adhered to within organizations.

1. Managers think members of their team are already operating at the outer limits of their potential.

    Sometimes managers think they've pushed their subordinates as far as they can push them, that they really are fully engaged and operating at their full potential. Sometimes this is an illusion shared by many in the organization.

    Managers overlooking the possibility of obtaining greater yields from available sources often fail to impose greater demands and expectations on their employees. When they do try to demand more, their subordinates are quick to point out they're doing all that can be done. Thus all levels of management may share the illusion of operating at the outer limit when, in fact, they are far from it.

—Robert H. Schaffer, *Harvard Business Review*

2. Both the leader and salesperson are afraid of failure.

    Fear of failure affects managers as well as the individuals on the team. The manager now not only fears for his own failure, but also feels responsible for the individual team members and the team as a whole. This fear may manifest itself by him either not setting goals and standards or not setting them high enough.

3. Higher standards equal more resistance.

    As a manager, the higher you set the bar, the more resistance you're going to get from the team. If you fear the push-back, you may keep the bar at too low a level simply to avoid resistance.

EXCELLENCE AND OBSTACLES

Standards that are casually set and lightly taken are freely abandoned at the first obstacle.
ZIG ZIGLAR

Unless you are extremely fortunate, every hour of every day, you and your team will experience obstacles like the lack of time, experience and resources, that will challenge your commitment to excellence.

Consider this short story. In 1968, a fire team of Marines was cut off from their unit. They were also dangerously low on ammunition in a firefight with the Viet Cong. The Marines quickly adapted; in between rifle shots, they began throwing rocks as though they were hand grenades.

The enemy fell back – many times. That bought the Marines enough time for support to arrive. That story is true, but the most inspirational thing about it is that it's not the first time Marines have thrown rocks at the enemy. They are taught to use whatever resources are available to them.

You and your team will continually experience challenges, but they will be successfully overcome when your commitment is stronger than the challenge. **You must rise above the resistance, defy the odds and set a new standard.**

Personal and business challenges are really opportunities in disguise. The larger your challenge the more you must grow and expand to solve it. While problems will never go away, the quality of your problems will get better as you get better.

What separates the top performers from those who struggle?

The way they handle obstacles. Average performers want everything to be easy. They see obstacles as annoying distractions. Top performers are simply more focused on successful outcomes. They see obstacles as opportunities to help them raise their level of play. They also see tougher obstacles and stronger opponents as opportunities to help them grow. That kind of thinking results in higher standards and better long-term results. Top performers take responsibility for results and remain ready for action.

In business, top performers see extra sales calls, continued learning and strategy sessions as their best friends. In sports, top performers see practice, drills and fundamentals as their best friends.

Consider Larry Bird. He was one of the world's all-time greatest professional basketball players. He was a man with average talent, but he was a man with a mile-high standard for results. That standard drove his behavior. He showed up early for practices and focused like a laser beam to perfect every movement. Next to him on the court were players with greater talent but lower standards. We remember him and have already forgotten them.

You see, top performers don't have jobs; they have careers. But more than just careers, they live lifestyles that are filled with achievement. **Top performers set high standards for dealing with problems. They set standards for what they will accept and expect from themselves and others.** They develop and maintain a positive outlook. However, they know that they must do much more than simply think in a positive way. They mobilize resources and prompt new solutions. Self-confidence and courage allow them to take responsibility for situations, and solve problems in a well-planned, organized way.

> *Ask yourself: What are my standards for dealing with problems? Do I accept "No" when I hear it, or do I find a way to "get to yes"? What are the highest standards that I will expect myself to live up to at all times in each area of my life?*

Establishing and living with higher personal standards can prove to be a tremendously liberating and results-changing decision. It will not only increase your revenue and results, but also help you experience more peace, contentment, and fulfillment.

ORGANIZATIONAL EXCELLENCE

> *We teach by what we do. What isn't so obvious is how many bad lessons we teach by what we allow. Every one of our actions sends a message to the people around us about our values, our standards, what we'll tolerate, and what we consider unacceptable.*
> ROB LEBOW AND WILLIAM L. SIMON
> *Lasting Change*

It's easy to have a standard and be committed to it as long as things are going your way. It's not so easy when faced with difficulties and obstacles. It is in these problematic situations that you will discover the true measure of an organization or individual's standards.

Here's a great example of a company that, when faced with a significant obstacle, decided to STEP UP! Members of the company proactively took responsibility and responded quickly and effectively to protect their customers. Rather than having a negative impact on profits, their behavior produced just the opposite.

In the Tylenol scare of 1982, seven people died in Chicago as a result of ingesting Tylenol capsules laced with cyanide. Evidence suggested the capsules had been taken from the store, tampered with, then returned to the shelf, i.e., it wasn't technically the fault of the manufacturer. Tylenol makers Johnson & Johnson could have easily shunned the blame and responsibility, but instead did exactly the opposite.

Johnson & Johnson's top management put customer safety first, before they worried about the company's profit and other financial concerns. **They stepped up and took full responsibility.** They immediately alerted consumers across the nation not to consume any type of Tylenol product. They told consumers not to resume using the product until the extent of the tampering could be determined. Johnson & Johnson also recalled all Tylenol capsules from the market. The recall included approximately 31 million bottles of Tylenol, with a retail value of more than 100 million dollars.

That is what I mean when I say, "Step Up!" On the other hand...

In many other crisis situations, companies made excuses and put themselves first, which produced a predictable result – greater damage to their reputations and their bottom line than if they had immediately taken responsibility for the crisis. Perrier is such a company.

Traces of benzene were found in Perrier bottled water. Instead of holding itself accountable for the incident, Perrier insisted that the contamination resulted from an isolated incident. The company recalled only a limited number of Perrier bottles in North America. By minimizing the danger, Perrier set a trap for itself and stumbled into it.

Benzene was found in Perrier bottled water in Europe. An embarrassed Perrier had to announce a worldwide recall on its bottled water. Apparently, consumers around the world had been drinking contaminated water for months. Perrier was harshly attacked by the media. The company was criticized for having little integrity and for disregarding public safety.

Let's look at the bottom line impact resulting from those two different approaches.

Johnson & Johnson showed its corporate values by protecting consumers first. The company did the right thing and got the right results. Its management chose to STEP UP. Financial damage from the Tylenol scare was minimized and Johnson & Johnson's behavior actually helped strengthen the brand and ensure future profitability.

Perrier's corporate values seemed to include self-serving and self-protection at a higher level than consumer safety. The company made excuses and failed to step up. Perrier lost market share and performance continues to lag. Where its bottled water once held top-of-mind recall before this crisis, it opened the door to competitors. Perrier has never recovered. For that, the company is forever regretful.

THE TOP VS. AVERAGE PERFORMERS

Average is being at the Top of the bottom!
MAMA

What separates Top Performers and those who struggle?

Top Performers push their upper limit in a self-motivated quest to be their best because they understand that excellence has no limits. In contrast, Average Performers have no upper limit because mediocrity is their best.

Top Performers are committed to mastery, while Average Performers are only interested in it. Top Performers set higher standards. Average Performers maintain existing standards. While others make excuses, Top Performers create results. They are proactive, not reactive. They consistently apply the principles of achievement, while others only occasionally do so.

Top Performers	Average Performers
Raise the Bar	"Settle" for Less
Take Responsibility	Make Excuses
Are Proactive	Are Reactive
Driven from Within	Externally Driven
Committed to Excellence	Interested in Excellence

THE KEY ACTION STEPS

Raise Your Standards

Here are the key action steps of this chapter:

1. Evaluate Your Standards

Identify an upcoming goal. Plot your commitment and confidence. Make the invisible more visible and make midcourse adjustments as needed.

2. Raise Your Standards

Set a higher standard for you and your teammates because the best results are always at the next level.

3. Buddy Up With the Best

Associate and surround yourself with people who have high standards. *How do you know who has high standards?* Simply look at their results. Identify three people or organizations that are achieving the results you'd like to achieve. Buddy up with them and you'll discover some of their recipes for results.

4. Take Responsibility for Results

It's easy to blame someone or something else for a lack of results, but in order to be a Top Performer you must STEP UP and be accountable. If you point blame, or deflect responsibility for a failure, you fail to learn from the mistakes. That's called "denial," and it's an ineffective strategy. Taking full responsibility for your Results is the ultimate standard. Just remember, when you point the finger at someone else you have three fingers pointing right back at you!

5. Eliminate Excuses

Eliminate the barriers that are limiting your individual and organizational results. Start by embracing the "Find a way or make a way" mindset.

IDENTIFY YOUR TALENTS

To be truly successful and achieve great results,
we must first fall in love with our work.
KAZUO INAMORI
A Passion for Success

Do You have the DNA for Results?

Every person is born with a one-of-a-kind biological DNA. DNA is your unique composition of internal factors that are responsible for the natural strengths and weaknesses within us.

Had you considered that you have a professional DNA, too?

You do. And it's equally as unique as your biological DNA. An organization has a collective DNA for Results. **A professional has an individual DNA for Results.** Superior results can be quickly achieved when your natural DNA is effectively aligned with the natural requirements of your job.

When there is a natural alignment you can achieve more results with fewer resources. Internal conflict will be reduced and external results will be increased because your passions, thinking and performance style will be a natural fit the job. You're positioned to achieve your maximum potential.

The DNA cell below illustrates that at the core of each individual and organization there is "natural genius." When you work in this nucleus you will do the right things, at the right times and produce the right results. You will achieve faster and go further because it is natural to you. Your professional work will become child's play.

THE DNA FOR RESULTS®

Geniuses have been studied extensively over the years. One of the most remarkable conclusions the researchers arrived at is that geniuses are not necessarily people with extraordinarily high IQs. They are often ordinary people who have aligned their natural DNA with career paths and goals that match their natural gifts. **What this means to you is that you can function at genius levels if you will step up, identify your natural talents and align them with a career path that rewards them.**

"You must become more authentic with yourself about yourself. You must know who you are at the core of your being. There you will find your genius. There you will find your passion. There you will find your calling."

If your job could talk, then what DNA would it demand for success in that position?

Do you honestly have that DNA?

SURRENDER TO YOUR PASSION

Regretfully, most people settle and "get a job" with a company to pay the bills. Too often their plan is to "get by" for 3 years, then depart the organization, so they can finally do what they really love to do. *Do you know of anyone like that?*

Top performing individuals reverse this order. They do what they love for a living from the beginning and it shows in their results. Their passion is their profession. *Are you doing what you love to do?*

Have you surrendered to your passion?

PERSONAL PASSION

Passion is the genesis of genius!
ANTHONY ROBBINS

With your permission, I'd like to share another sliver of my personal story with you, because it illustrates the importance of surrendering to your professional passions.

After graduating with my MBA, I entered Corporate America. I "got a job" in the railroad industry and began my selling career. *Why railroading?* Point blank, I needed a job! I had bills to pay. *Have you ever been there? Still there?*

My plan was to create value for my employer and achieve superior results. And initially, I was successful. *Why?* Well, there were several reasons, but the biggest reason was that I went to work on myself. I heard someone say "If you want to be successful, then study success." So, I did. I began reading voraciously. And as a result, I started to STEP UP.

At work, I received public praise. But at home, I endured private pain. *Why?* Well, I loved selling, but I didn't love the railroad industry. Sure I liked it, but I didn't love it. In time, I became disengaged and it showed in my results.

You see, creating and sustaining superior results requires a genuine match between your personal passions and the job. People who are genuinely passionate about their position and company go further and achieve results faster because they love what they do for a living. They've got the ultimate competitive advantage. In short, **passion propels and pretending repels results.** *Are you passionate or pretending in your career?*

As Mama used to say, "You've gotta love it or leave it alone!" I could no longer pretend that I loved something that I didn't. While I was uncertain about what the future held for me, I had to STEP UP. *What happened to me next?* More about me later, for now let's return to our broader discussion about talents.

THE DNA FOR RESULTS

Success in Sales is 80% nature and 20% nurture.
DANIEL GRISSOM

Does success in sales originate from nature or nurture?

I believe it's mostly a function of nature. You must have many natural instincts to be a top performer. Of course, even top performers must nurture these talents, but sales success is in their blood. *Do you have the DNA to achieve superior results in sales?*

Consider these definitions for *natural – produced by nature, not acquired, by blood rather than adoption; instinctive, God-given.* Now, compare that with the definitions for *nurture – the act of learning and educating oneself; to attempt to develop; cultivate, breed or strengthen.* From these definitions you can see that achieving superior results is a natural outcome if you have the natural talent.

Regretfully, **most of us take jobs that rely heavily on the nurturing of our talents rather than unleashing our natural talents.** *Why is that?*

Consider this excerpt from *The Power of College Students* (HCI, 2005) and the potential root causes for such behavior:

> *Somewhere between childhood and the real world one of two things happen, either you start to follow the dreams of your parents, your neighbors or someone else or you get caught up in pursuing the dollars and status associated with a certain career. People who do this leave their passion on a shelf collecting dust and end up becoming part of the 70% of professionals who dislike what they do.*

The fact is that creating and sustaining competitive advantage originates from a superior alignment between your natural DNA and the job. Consider Michael Jordan as a parallel to the corporate athlete in business. Jordan had amazing natural DNA for basketball, but when he tried to transfer these same gifts to baseball, he became just another average player. Jordan mismatched his natural DNA with the natural requirements of the job and it showed in his results. As the corporate athlete, *could you have the right DNA, but be playing in the wrong sport (industry)?*

Let's continue with the parallel. Jordan was a 10 time All-Star playing the shooting guard position. But, *would his results have been as prolific had he moved to the center position?* No, because he would have been playing out of position, which would have affected his results. He would have been good, but not great. As the corporate athlete, *could you be playing out of position? Is there a better fit for you in marketing or customer service?*

So, does this mean that having the right DNA for the position guarantees superior results? No, it does not. You must build upon your natural talents. *Did you know that Jordan failed to make his high school basketball team, initially?* That's right, even though he had the natural talent for the sport, Jordan had to nurture these gifts to win a spot on the team the next season. As sellers and leaders, the same is true for us. We may have the right DNA, and we may be in the right position, but we still must nurture our talents to produce the right results. As the corporate athlete, *what areas of your professional game should you nurture to achieve superior results?*

Last, while Jordan's superb shooting and playmaking skills may have been from nurture, his inner drive and competitive instincts were from nature. And these natural talents were his ultimate competitive edge. You see, **your natural DNA is your competitive advantage in today's marketplace.** You must identify it, align it and unleash it. **There is a part of you that is destined for greatness.** *Have you unleashed it?*

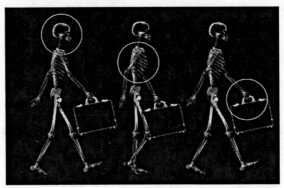

As the visual above illustrates, your DNA can be identified by examining three dimensions – your head, heart and hand. In other words, with the latest in assessments, we can examine or x-ray how you think, what motivates you and how you handle situations. If you would like to identify your individual DNA or organizational DNA, then drop me an email at **daniel@phdinresults.com**. I'll give you with a complimentary examination.

TALENTS OR DNA:

- Drive profits
- Your natural style fits
- Enable you to achieve more with less

IF YOUR JOB COULD TALK

If either organizational fit or job fit is unsatisfactory, it is almost impossible to increase performance with training or coaching.
CHUCK RUSSELL
Right Person – Right Job

There is no right or wrong DNA. There is best fit. *If your job could talk, then what would it say about the DNA required for success in your current position? How strong of a match is there between your DNA and the requirements of that position?*

Success in your job requires a successful match between the natural requirements of the job and your natural DNA.

If the Job Could Talk?

Think about it. If you have more talent than the job rewards, then you will find yourself bored and unfulfilled, which leads to attrition. If you have less talent than the job requires, you will find yourself making errors, which leads to unemployment. **An authentic match between your natural genius and the natural demands of the job positions you for superior results.** That's because you'll be able to tap into your natural talent to achieve your goals. You'll have more drive and experience less drama. Your organization will experience less talent turnover and more employee engagement. In short, you and your organization can create a sustainable, competitive advantage because your team will have the right players in the right positions doing the right things and producing the right results. *Isn't that the essence of success for all championship teams?*

Consider the *Harvard Business Review* study that determined in approximately 300,000 cases that the only statistically significant difference in job performance and results was "Job Match." The conclusion was that "It's not experience that counts or college degrees or other accepted factors; success on the job hinges on a fit with the job."[8]

Align your DNA to make more M.O.N.E.Y.

THE UNCOMMON DENOMINATOR

Like everyone else, I've got the same trucks. Like everyone else, I've got the same potatoes. Like everyone else, I've got the same machinery. The only thing I can have different is better people.
HERMAN LAY
Founder of Frito-Lay

Let's face it. For products and services, in every industry, commoditization is a problem. Even the most talented individuals and organizations are struggling with it.

While your company is developing sales strategies to increase your revenue, many of your clients are creating purchasing strategies to crush your plans and drive value to the lowest common denominator – price.

Take a look at the graphic on the right. It identifies the common denominators in business. Consider the fact that

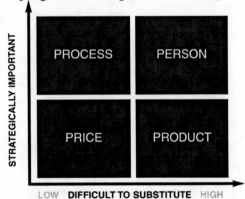

---

8. *Harvard Business Review, Job Matching for Better Sales Performance*

your competitors can easily match your price. They can easily mirror your product/service. And even though your processes are valuable, they too can be duplicated with the right people. The sustainable competitive advantage of any team and organization is its people. If you're on top of your game, then you have successfully positioned yourself to be strategically important and difficult to substitute to your clients and organization.

YOU are the uncommon denominator. You make the difference in creating client value, advancing the sales cycle and achieving competitive advantage. I've seen this ring true time and time again. Clients choose one supplier over another based solely on the people involved. *Want an example?* Then fast forward to my experience with Google in the Unleash Potential chapter (section titled "Personal Power").

HIRING TOP TALENT

You want to hire people with an MBA in their DNA.
DANIEL GRISSOM

As we discussed earlier, the market has stepped up. Tangible assets like technology, real estate, facilities, even investments and cash are no longer differentiators. They are basic requirements to meet the minimum standards. The real value now comes from intangibles such as brand identification and loyalty, client relationships, intellectual property, and the biggest and most valuable intangible – people.

According to a study conducted by a team from McKinsey & Company, the most important corporate resource over the next 20 years will be talent: smart, sophisticated businesspeople that are technologically literate, globally astute and operationally agile.

Therefore, **the most important breakthrough for a business is in knowing how to match talent with the requirements of the job.** Yet, one of the biggest and most costly errors organizations make is placing the right people in the wrong positions.

———•———

Superior talent is often the difference between winning and losing in sales and leadership.

This mistake takes these forms. The organization:

1. Doesn't have the right talent.

2. Has the right talent, but has placed it in the wrong position (job or role).

3. Has the right talent in the right position, but fails to develop the talent to ensure the right things get done.

What if your organization could improve its talent selection effectiveness by 10%?

What effect would it have on your organization's value?

Here's what that would look like:

Market Value	Market Value Improvement
$1M	$100K
$100M	$10M
$1B	$100M

TOP TALENT TURBULENCE

People first, strategy and everything else second.
JACK WELCH
Straight From the Gut

The more effective an organization is at hiring, developing and retaining talent the more successful that organization will be at achieving its goals and increasing its revenues. That's synergy, which can be illustrated like this: 1 + 1 = 3.

There's alchemy in hiring, developing and retaining top performers. In other words, talent plus the personal growth of the individuals in the organization drive business prosperity. That's how it's supposed to work.

However, when the organization neglects to hire the best talent, or fails to develop it, a dysfunctional culture of mediocrity and turnover takes root. Let's call it "reverse alchemy." Where "alchemy" is the magical result of the combination equaling something greater than the sum of the parts, **reverse alchemy refers to a corporate culture in which the whole equals less than the sum of the parts.**

Picture it like this: 1 + 1 = 1

Larry Bossidy in his best-selling book *Execution* discusses the impact that talent selection has on results:

Hiring results probably won't show up as quickly as say a big acquisition. But over time, choosing the right people is what creates that elusive competitive advantage.[9]

If you look at any business that's consistently successful, **you'll find that its leaders focus intensely and relentlessly on people selection.**

The foundation of a great organization is the way it develops people. If you spend the same amount of time and energy developing people as

---

9. *Execution: The Discipline of Getting Things Done* by Larry Bossidy, Ram Charan, Charles Burck

you do on budgeting, strategic planning and financial monitoring, the payoff will come in sustainable competitive advantage.

Failure to hire or develop talent is probably the worst mistake possible for a firm wanting to succeed. It also affects the stock value of the business as evidenced by an Ernst & Young study.

E&Y looked at what analysts use as the basis for making buy or sell recommendations. The study revealed that 35% of an investment decision is driven by consideration of non-financial data – things like the Ability to Attract Talented People, Leadership Credibility, and Reputation.[10]

Although we often think of companies as monolithic entities, they're not. They're collections of individuals who typically act in their own self-interest. Superior and consistent corporate execution occurs only when the actions of individuals within an organization are aligned with one another and when the overall strategic interests and values of the company. Performance is the sum total of the tens of thousands of actions and decisions that, at large companies, thousands of people at every level make every day as pointed out by Booz-Allen in its Resilience Report.[11]

BLIND SPOTS

I predict that within the next 5 years, the ability to retain employees and maintain a stable workforce will become the primary competitive advantage for organizations.
ROER HERMAN
Futurist

Bias is an unfair preference or dislike of something. Bias can create a blind spot – blocking out a single thing – or acting like a set of blinders

10. E&Y Study, *What Analysts Look at to Make Buy Sell Recommendations*
11. Booz Allen, *Organizational DNA, The Resilience Report*

– making only one thing visible. Unfortunately, biases get in the way of truly understanding job requirements and talent fit.

A three-year study of 5,247 hiring managers by Leadership IQ, a leadership and training firm, revealed that **46% of newly-hired employees will fail within their first year and one half of employment.**[10]

The typical interview process fixates on ensuring new hires are technically competent. The problem is that technical skills or industry experience are not a sufficient measure of one's capability to do a job. Although the primary focus in most interviews is technical skills, skill level ends up being one of the last reasons people lose their jobs.

The factors that do dramatically affect a person's effectiveness in a job are: coachability, emotional intelligence, motivation and temperament. Furthermore, consider this research concerning the effectiveness of many organizations' talent selection systems:

Interviews are only 14% accurate in predicting success on the job. The root cause for inaccuracies: personal bias.

—Michigan State University

Two of three hires prove to be bad fits within the first year.

—The Harvard Business Review

The cost of a hiring mistake is 3x the employee's salary.

—The Gallup Organization

How effective is your organization's system for hiring top sales talent?

Could your personal biases be impacting your business results?

I QUIT, BUT YOU'RE STILL PAYING ME!

———————

Success without fulfillment is failure.
TONY ROBBINS

If your organization is pretty good at hiring talent, then celebrate that fact. Then, get ready for another reality check. **A study by the Gallup organization found that 75% of the employees in most companies are not engaged at work.**

A disengaged professional is one that is going through the motions (movement), but the emotions (achievement) aren't going through them. They are making a living, instead of designing a destiny. The effect: Not only are disengaged employees not making you any money, they're costing you money because they're the ones making all the mistakes!

Gallup's Coffman and Gabriel Gonzalez-Molina tell us:

"Disengaged employees cost companies hundreds of millions of dollars a year."

They estimate lost productivity cost at $3,400 per $10,000 of salary. **That means a $100,000 disengaged employee costs you $34,000 a year in lost productivity.** And that's only if he doesn't make any really costly mistakes. Remember, that's not a one-time cost; it's an ongoing one.

Finally, **the cost of an organizational leader being disengaged is likely three times that of an employee.** *Why?* Because leaders have higher salaries and have a multiplier effect on the rest of the organization. When leaders are misaligned they are likely to hire and lead ineffectively.[12]

What is the primary cause of disengagement?

The primary cause of employee disengagement is poor job fit. More specifically, people in jobs that don't make use of their natural talents or

———————

12. *Follow This Path: How the World's Greatest Organizations Drive Growth* by Unleashing Human Potential, Curt Coffman and Gabriel Gonzalez-Molina, Ph.D

genius. **Bad job fit causes turnover, job stress and stress causes absenteeism and accidents.**

Gallup found that employees who are able to utilize their natural talents or genius in their jobs are more likely to be engaged. Not only are engaged employees significantly more productive, but they also impact the bottom line in other important ways. They don't make costly mistakes. They recognize and capitalize on opportunities. They create "engaged clients" which experts claim is key to driving sustainable growth, in all organizations across all industries.[11]

RIGHT PERSON. RIGHT JOB. BAD FIT?

If we get the right people on the bus, the right people in the right seats and the wrong people off the bus, then we'll figure out how to take it someplace great.
JIM COLLINS
Good to Great

So, you've got the right talent in the right job. The person and the position are a match. Your mission is accomplished, *right*? Wrong!

What about your corporate culture?

Does your talent fight it or fit it?

Your culture is the collection of the individual DNA within the organization. So let's call it organizational DNA. **Let's examine two examples of the right person, right job, but a bad fit.**

First story. Very few sports fans today remember the name Joe Don Looney. One sportswriter described him as "the greatest player who

---

13. *ibid.*

never was." Looney was the star of the Oklahoma Sooners under Bud Wilkinson in 1962-63. He made a huge difference in performance on the field. However, he hung onto a terrible work ethic.

Looney once said, "A good running back makes his own holes. Anybody can run where the holes are." That was his way of explaining why he missed practice and refused to learn the playbook. *How would you like that kind of an influence on your team?* The team didn't like it. Looney was kicked off. He was the right person in the right position, but a bad fit.

Second story. In 2004-05 Terrell Owens was the star, All Pro wide receiver for the Philadelphia Eagles. Like Joe Don Looney, Owens was the right person, right position, but a bad fit for his team. The decision makers for the Eagles followed in Bud Wilkinson's footsteps. They kicked Owens off the team.

On November 5, 2005, with two months left in the season, the star receiver was suspended after criticizing quarterback Donovan McNabb and calling the organization "classless." That was bad enough, but it got worse. Owens and the Eagles went into arbitration – another destructive distraction to the team – to settle the dispute. Ultimately, the arbitrator upheld the team's decision, saying that Owens' conduct was a "destructive and continuing threat" to his team.

Get it? Joe Don Looney and Terrell Owens had the right talent for the position, but were bad fits for those cultures. They did more damage than good. *If you had been the decision maker in those situations, would you have had the wisdom to let them go?* My guess is you would if you understood the value of your culture and the serious wounds that a mismatch can inflict on it. However, if you've fallen into the trap of sacrificing the future success for immediate gains, you may have retained Looney or Owens.

ORGANIZATIONAL DNA

*No company can expect to beat the competition unless it has the
best human capital and promotes these people to pivotal positions.*
LARRY BOSSIDY
Former Chairman of Honeywell

Each year companies set goals and make promises to Wall Street investment firms. Fortunately for us, analysts and investors love to investigate.
One of their principal investigative questions is, *"Does this company's culture (organizational DNA) align with its goals?"* **When there's a gap
between an organization's natural talents and its goals, Wall Street pun-
ishes it with a deep dip in stock price.** *Why?* Because Wall Street knows
that company culture is an accurate predictor of performance.

Business researchers agree: organizations benefit from having highly
motivated employees dedicated to common goals. The performance benefits of a strong corporate culture derive from three consequences of having
widely shared and strongly held norms and values:

1. Enhanced coordination and control within the firm.

2. Improved goal alignment between the firm and its members.

3. Increased employee effort.

MAJOR LEAGUE LESSONS

I believe there are many parallels between sports and business. And
frankly I believe there are many valuable lessons to be learned by observing the do's and don'ts of professional franchises concerning the hiring,
developing and retaining of talent.

For example, take the NBA. Each new season a team has the opportunity to draft new players, develop existing players and trade or retire
others. *What criteria do they use to hire, develop and retain talent?* First,

they draft players that have the DNA to be top performers. Second, they look for players whose attitude and mental toughness fit within their system and culture.

Yet, most NBA franchises have a low success rate in effectively drafting or trading for the right players at the right time to win championships. *Why is that?*

The problem starts with their selection and evaluation process. Consider the similarities between an NBA team and a Fortune 100 Corporation.

1. NBA teams conduct scouting reports. Corporations conduct background checks.

2. NBA teams watch the videotape of a player's previous performance. Corporations look at samples of the talent's work.

3. NBA teams talk with former coaches. Corporations talk with former managers.

4. NBA teams look at the player's stat sheets. Corporations examine the talent's degrees and resumes.

Both groups conduct rigorous research, but most of it is superficial. All their research and data is centered on skills and characteristics. But as I explain in the next section, **you must make the invisible visible.** You must examine the factors that are most important for results (DNA, heart, psychology, mental make-up, standards). This is true when a corporation hires the corporate athlete, too.

Sure, a sports team may have the player take a basic physical or have an X-ray, but it doesn't measure the heart, the mind or commitment to excellence. As a result, **many teams and organizations inadvertently filter in the wrong talent andfilter out the right talent.**

Consider the fact that Michael Jordan was drafted third when he graduated from college and entered the NBA. *Why wasn't he drafted #1?* Because the surface level scouting report was based on factors above the iceberg, not those factors below the surface – his heart or mental commitment to excellence.

Who was drafted #1 and what happened to him? His name was Sam Bowie. He played for three seasons, got hurt and retired. *Do people today even remember Bowie? The cost of this talent misread?* Six championships, a legacy/brand and trillions of dollars. This happens in corporations, too. It's just not tracked as well – the cost of hiring the wrong talent and the opportunity cost of missing the right talent or the cost of misreading talent regarding promotions and retention!

So, what's the solution?

LOOK BELOW THE SURFACE

Today it is not necessary to accept the risk of marginal results that are inherent in traditional hiring methods.
CHUCK RUSSELL
Right Person – Right Job

Two-thirds of your hiring decision should be based on your observations above the surface, like interviews, resumes and references. The remaining one-third of the decision should be based on observation obtained below the surface. The difference between what you see and what you need to see can make the difference between hiring a top performer or an underperformer.

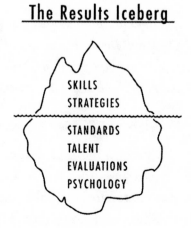

The Results Iceberg

SKILLS
STRATEGIES

STANDARDS
TALENT
EVALUATIONS
PSYCHOLOGY

You need to know that your players will be committed, passionate, possess high standards and have the mental horsepower to be Top Performers. And you want to discover this sooner, rather than later, because time is money.

Amazingly, many organizations are unaware of the accuracy and efficiency with which we can quickly examine, analyze and profile talent – inside and out. Using better technology and assessments, we can compress decades of observation into days. The result is you gain insight into your talent for hiring, developing, coaching and retaining. **The STEP UP model focuses below the iceberg where you find substance and significance.** That's where the greatest return is.

HOW TO HIRE TOP TALENT

1. **Make Effective Talent Selection the Priority.**

   Consider these comments from Larry Bossidy in *Execution*:

   Hiring results probably won't show up as quickly as say a big acquisition. But over time, choosing the right people is what creates that elusive competitive advantage.

   If you look at any business that's consistently successful, you'll find that its leaders focus intensely and relentlessly on people selection.

   The foundation of a great company is the way it develops people. If you spend the same amount of time and energy developing people as you do on budgeting, strategic planning and financial monitoring, the payoff will come in sustainable competitive advantage.

2. **Develop an Effective Talent Selection System.**

   Top performing organizations first benchmark the job and identify the key characteristics required for success in that job. Then they assess the candidates for the sales position and identify their sales DNA. Finally, they compare the candidates against the key characteristics. The individual whose DNA most closely aligns with the requirements of the job is the candidate of choice.

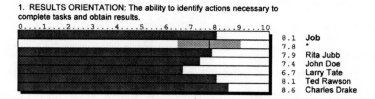

8.1	**Job**
7.8	*
7.9	Rita Jubb
7.4	John Doe
6.7	Larry Tate
8.1	Ted Rawson
8.6	Charles Drake

3. Develop an Effective Talent Management System.

An effective performance management system enables organizations to customize their professional development to the specific needs of each employee, which leads to greater productivity, less turnover and higher profitability.

PERFORMANCE REVIEWS

Very few companies have meaningful evaluation systems in place.
That's not just bad – it's terrible!
JACK WELCH
Winning

Perhaps the single most important assessment an organization makes is the evaluation of its existing talent. Every manager makes evaluations, and every employee gets evaluated.

There are two types of performance reviews. The first is a formal appraisal usually conducted every six to 12 months. The other is informal which is day-to-day feedback and coaching. **These evaluations or reviews should be inextricably linked to organizational strategy, but so often are not.**

This is detrimental to performance and profits because these reviews provide the raw material for individuals and organizations to make effective mid-course corrections. Moreover, the typical performance review seems to be more about human resource administration than human capital maximization. And the typical performance review tends to be subjective and infrequent rather than objective and consistent.

Jack Welch crystallizes this point in his book *Winning*, where he points out that he often asks his audiences, *"How many of you have received an honest, straight-between-the-eyes feedback session in the past year, where you came out knowing exactly what you have to do to improve and where you stand in the organization?"* Only 20% of the audience raises its hand on a good day, but the average yes response is about 10%. If this unscientific research is anywhere near correct, **very few companies have meaningful evaluation systems in place.** That's not just bad – it's terrible!"[14]

Welch goes on to say how nice it would be if performance evaluations were done with the same rigor as financial evaluations. After all, financial results are because of people. **Sadly, performance evaluation systems are often just exercises in paper pushing.**

Effective professional development reviews are precursors to effective business development results. You cannot have one without the other.

THE TOP VS. AVERAGE PERFORMERS

Average is being at the Top of the bottom!
MAMA

What separates Top Performers from those who struggle?

Top Performers align their DNA with the job. This effective alignment is by choice while Average Performers often align by chance. Average

---

14. *Winning* by Jack Welch, Suzy Welch

Performers have the potential to become Top Performers, NOT by investing in more skills training, but by aligning with a position that best matches their DNA for Results.

Top Performers align their DNA with careers that tap into their natural genius, which creates unlimited potential.

Average Performers try to fit into existing jobs and situations, which limit their potential.

Top Performers are internally driven. They take responsibility for identifying, understanding and leveraging their natural talents. Average Performers tend to look to and wait for external sources to "define" and guide them.

Top Performers step up to the challenge and differentiate themselves, while Average Performers depend on the product or service to differentiate them.

Here's a summary:

Top Performers	Average Performers
Fit the Job	Fight the Job
Unlimited Potential	Limited Potential
Desire to Win	Desire to Play
Internally Driven	Externally Defined
Step Up	Back Down

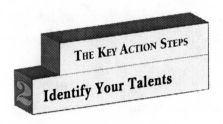

THE KEY ACTION STEPS

Identify Your Talents

Here are the key action steps of this chapter:

1. **Discover Your Natural Genius.**

    Learn who you are rather than telling yourself who you should be. Then, align your genius with the career path or goals that reward it. Superior alignment produces superior results.

2. **Invest in Your #1 Product – YOU!**

    Face it, your results will grow only to the extent that you do.

3. **Prioritize Talent Selection and Development.**

4. **Improve Your Talent Selection System.**

    Increase retention and reduce turnover by ensuring that two-thirds of your hiring decisions are based on subjective insight like interviews, resumes and experience. One-third of your hiring decision should be based on objective data via the use of assessments.

5. **Improve the Quality and Consistency of Your Performance Reviews.**

    Feedback enables mid-course corrections and helps improve performance.

Step Three

CONSISTENT SELF-EVALUATION

Self Evaluation is the 1st Chapter in the Book of Wisdom.
MAMA

Is your work and life in balance?

Top performing individuals and organizations achieve a balance between their professional pursuits and personal interests. They understand that their *drive to achieve* excellence in business is secondary to their primary *desire to realize* happiness in life. *Have your been getting the order reversed?*

Excellence invites us to consistently evaluate ourselves. It encourages us to search for a healthy balance between business and life. Consider the diagram below. It identifies and organizes the six major aspects of life. It illustrates that your fulfillment in your personal life is inextricably linked to achievement in your professional career.

Think about it. You wouldn't want to step up your career and lose your health. Nor would you want to step up in your business and lose your health, family and relationship with God. *Does that make sense?* For peak performers, the priorities are **God first, family second and career third**.

In short, you can achieve bigger results when you achieve better balance. This begins with consistent self evaluation and measurement. And, **you can't manage what you don't measure**.

> ### EVALUATIONS ARE:
> - Mental work you do prior to making a decision.
> - Sets of habitual questions you ask prior to taking action.
> - Tools to close the results gap.

THE KING OF EVALUATIONS

Wisdom is supreme; Though it may cost all you have,
get understanding.
PROVERBS 4:7

The Bible teaches us that there once was a king that was given the opportunity to ask and receive anything from the Giver of Life. That's right, absolutely anything! *Well, what did he ask for?* He asked for wisdom. *But, why wisdom?* After all, he could have asked for more revenue, more relationships or more results. **It's because he understood that wisdom is supreme.**

What's wisdom? It's the ability to understand what's true and right. It's the ability to develop insight into problems and possible solutions. **It's the power to conduct superior evaluations.** As a result, the king became the wisest and most intelligent man on earth.

If you were given the opportunity to ask for anything, *what would you ask for? More revenue, relationships or results?* **We should ask for more** business wisdom, which is the power to conduct superior evaluations. It's the essence of success.

PERSONAL EVALUATION

Whatever games are played with us, we must
play no games with ourselves.
MAMA

Introspection – **the ability to go on the inside, so you can grow on the outside**. *How introspective are you?* With your permission, I'd like to share another sliver of my personal story, because it illustrates how your self talk affects your focus and results.

It was 1999 and I decided to STEP UP and depart the railroad industry. I landed a sweet job with a transportation software company. And although **this position was still not my ultimate dream job**, it was a better fit than railroading.

He who walks in the middle of the road gets hit from both sides.
GEORGE SCHULTZ

And then what happened? Well, six months after accepting this new job, the employer eliminated it, along with others and filed for bankruptcy. **I got downsized. The bottom fell out and my mouth flew open!** This hurt, but the worst wounds were self-inflicted. I began asking myself questions like "*Why did they do this to me?*" and "*What's wrong with them?*" These questions were disempowering because they inferred that someone else controlled my destiny. They were "others-focused" questions.

Then? I started substitute teaching to earn money, while I evaluated my options. Over time, I began to upgrade the quality of my questions. I began asking *"What comes easily to me, but difficult to others? What actions should I take to step up to the next level?"* Unlike the former questions, these questions were empowering because they affirmed that I was the director of my destiny. These were "self-focused" questions. *Are your current questions empowering or disempowering you?* You see, achieving superior results begins with an honest evaluation of ourselves and the way we communicate with ourselves.

I knew I had to step up and **start living more authentically**. My *professional* passions were in the field of Training and Development. So, I tried promoting seminars with the Tony Robbins organization. This was good, but not great. **I was rich with passion, but miserable with no money.**

Then? I heard about **Huthwaite**, the premiere provider of consultative sales training and makers of Spin® selling. They were the **Harvard University of Sales** and they had a job vacancy and were hiring sales consultants. This fit my "DNA to a T." This was my dream job!

And so, I prepared well for the interview. The first interview went great and I was invited back. Again, I prepared well and the second interview went great too. *Did I get the position?* Much to my chagrin, I did not. Huthwaite informed me that I was not a fit for their sales force. I was crushed. My mission to secure my dream job had turned into a nightmare.

What happened next? Well, we'll return to the next step in my story in the following chapter For now, let's return to our broader discussion on evaluations.

QUESTIONS ARE THE ANSWER

He who asks questions cannot avoid answers.
CHINESE PROVERB

A fascinating thing about the questions we ask ourselves is their ability to influence our actions and results. Think about it. Your questions reflect your thinking. The answers govern your options. They determine your actions and your actions drive results.

When you focus on a desired result, your mind produces ideas and questions. Here's an example – If I focus on closing the deal, then my self-talk or inner questions are primarily related to closing the deal. For example, I'll focus on questions like: *How can I get them to sign on the dotted line? How much money will I make if they choose this option over that option? Which closing technique should I use?*

If those are my questions and focus, then my actions will be in alignment with them. I will focus on doing whatever I need to get them to sign on the dotted line. What I won't even think of are questions that probe the client's experience. *How can I create more client value? What's best for the client? What solutions can I provide to the client's challenges?*

Are your current questions good or bad? Well, that depends on your desired results. Examine your current results and your internal dialogue. *Are your questions serving you or sabotaging you?*

By improving the questions you and your organization ask, you can control focus, influence action and drive better results. If you want results no one else has, then ask questions no one else thinks to ask!

EVALUATE YOUR COMMUNICATION

Think like a man of action and act like a man of thought.
HENRI BERGSON

The questions you ask yourself each day influence your focus, which drives your behavior and results. Your thoughts create your reality. In other words, **what you focus on grows**.

Here's an example of a salesperson's self-talk and probable actions and results:

Questions	Action	Results
How can I make the sale and get my money?	• Saying and doing whatever it takes to get the prospect to say yes	• Minimal customer satisfaction • Transactional sale • Assuming value and forcing a "close"
How can I create value for the client?	• Taking the time to understand the client's needs • Continually looking for ways to add value	• Maximum client satisfaction • Stronger, more profitable relationships
How many sales have we made this month?	• Saying and doing whatever it takes to up the sales numbers • Lots of reports and measures that look at sales	• Transactional sales approach • Short-term results • Sacrificing easier future sales for lower-quality immediate ones
How can we ensure our employees are fully engaged?	• Coaching our team members to ensure they advance from good to GREAT • Customizing our training to our talent's specific needs • Measuring the results of client engagements	• Strategic employee development and retention • Stronger, more profitable client relationships • Long-term results • A corporate culture based on constant improvement

*Your results are often
related to the questions you ask and fail to ask.*

THE CORE QUESTION

The way a man's mind runs is the way he is sure to go.
HENRY WILSON

The daily or core questions that we ask ourselves reflect our personal passions and desires. They influence our daily behavior. Here's how it works.

If our self-talk or inner questions are about closing the deal, then that's obviously what we value most. If on the other hand, they are about understanding the client and creating value for them, then that's illustrative of a different set of values.

Your core questions filter most, if not all, of the evaluations in your life. It's the one question you most frequently ask yourself. For instance, my primary question is *How can I improve?* My wife Taisia's is *How can I have fun?* My business partner Pam's is *What can I learn?* Each of us has a different core question that dramatically influences our evaluations and decisions. *How does this play out?*

Taisia filters for fun which means she's continually looking for situations that provide fun. Pam filters for learning which means she'll seek out and make decisions based on the opportunity to learn and grow. As for me, I'm all about results, so I look for ways I can personally improve or ways I can improve the results of my clients. *What's your core question?*

Although there is no right or wrong question, it's fair to say some questions produce better results than others at least in particular situations.

Here's an example. An event planner whose core question is *How can I have fun or help other people have fun?* would do much better than one whose primary question is *What can I learn?*

A consultative sales person whose primary question is *How can I add value?* or *How can I produce results?* will do better than one who's primary question is *How can I have fun?* or *What can I learn?*

Although each of us has core internal questions, the questions we ask are contextual. My primary personality may be one of filtering for learning, but I recognize that in a sales situation, the more effective questions are those related to creating value for the customer.

So what do I do? Simple. I combine my primary filter for learning with adding value for the customer. The new question then becomes — *What can I learn that I can use to create value for my customer?* For Taisia in a sales situation, the new question might be *How can I have fun creating value for my customer?*

You see, your questions mirror your core values. *What question do you subconsciously ask yourself each day?* The answer will reveal the driving force within you.

QUALITY OF QUESTIONS

There are two voices in your head — one is always wrong.
KAREN CASEY

You can improve your results by asking better questions. One of the ways you can do this is to ask *How* rather than *Why, When* or *Who* questions. The reason is only the *How* questions get you focused on the possibilities. The other questions get you focused on the problems. For example:

Rather than ask — *Why are we behind in our sales plan?*

Better to ask – *How can we improve our sales forecasting process?*

Rather than ask – *Who is responsible for cutting the price to close the deal?*

Better to ask – *How can we help our sellers effectively communicate our value proposition?*

Recently, I read a story about Bill Gates. Apparently, Gates asked himself some empowering questions every day like, *"What's impossible to do in my industry today? What's currently impossible that I could do that would change the quality of my business, revolutionize the industry and improve my results forever?"* Now, think of what Bill Gates started to notice and focus on as he continued to ask himself these questions. He started to see not necessarily what was impossible, but what was possible!

In short, **questions influence what you see and don't see**. It's not only the questions you ask, but the questions that you *fail* to ask that determine your results. Again, **if you want results no one else is getting, then start asking questions no one else is asking.**

THE RESULTS GAP

At the end of each day, you should play back the tapes of your performance. Your results should either applaud you or prod you.
JIM ROHN

How often should you evaluate your results?

Well, that depends. It depends on how often you want to achieve superior results. If you want to consistently achieve the best results, then you must consistently evaluate and measure your performance. *Why?* Because **too much time elapsed between measurements often translates into lost opportunities and inferior results.** The longer you wait the greater your risk.

There are three key questions you should ask yourself at the end of each day, or at least once a week, to improve your performance and results.

Key Questions

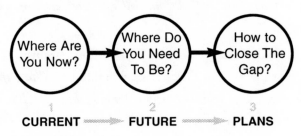

Think about the investors on Wall Street. They must make effective evaluations and keep score every moment of every day. They are disciplined in asking themselves, *"How's my investment doing today? Should I buy, hold or sell to improve results? What actions should I take to close the gap between my actual and potential results?"*

The Results Gap

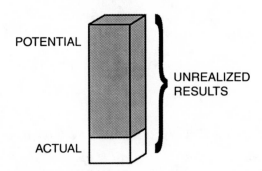

These daily questions help them to keep score, make mid-course corrections and take the right actions to close the results gap. Consider modeling this behavior to improve your performance and results. After all, you are human capital. You are the ultimate asset in business. *Are you measuring the performance of your portfolio (stocks, bonds and 401k) more frequently than your personal performance?*

THE DNA OF GOOD DECISION-MAKING

Simple is smart.
MAMA

You evaluate options and make decisions every day. Often these evaluations are made quickly and subconsciously. *Should I take action today or tomorrow? Should I invest my time doing expense reports or planning for an upcoming sales call? Which sales strategy will work best?*

We often don't realize we're making decisions, weighing options and doing the necessary mental work in order to make the best choice. This lack of awareness contributes to the lack of results.

My aim is **to bring the invisible (unconscious process) clearly into your conscious minds,** so that you can purposefully and proactively ask the best questions and make decisions that ensure the best results.

Here are the smart, but simple steps for good decision-making:

1. Separate facts from feelings and analyze the facts.
2. Think on paper and identify the key issues or opportunities.
3. Evaluate your options, select the best option and take immediate action.

You can't get to the next level of results with the same level of thinking.

EXCELLENCE IN EVALUATIONS

Excellence begins with you!
DANIEL GRISSOM

Over the last 15 years as I've been teaching people how to make sound evaluations, I've noticed a consistency. It deals with where people begin their evaluations. Top Performers begin with themselves and Average Performers begin with the organization.

For example, starting at the bottom, top performers ask, *"How can I make a difference for my team and organization?"* Starting at the top, with the organization Average Performers ask, *"How can my organization make a difference to me?"* The most effective evaluation is to begin with yourself, then examine your team and organization.

Evaluating yourself or your organization means realistically looking within and identifying not only strengths, but also weaknesses. Most individuals and organizations are good at identifying strengths, but not always so good at identifying weaknesses. Remember Garrison Keeler's Lake Wobegon community, "where the women are strong, the men are good-looking, and all the children are above average." It seems we all tend to suffer from the Lake Wobegon effect where we see ourselves better than we really are.

*The **Lake Wobegon effect**, also called **better-than-average effect**, is a term used by psychologists to refer to the human tendency to report flattering beliefs about oneself and believe that one is above average. Many experiments have shown that most people believe that they possess more desirable attributes than other people.*
(From Wikipedia)

Countless studies looking at everything from driving to getting along with other people show that most people rank themselves better than average, even though statistically this is impossible.

In a study by Ola Svenson, 80% of students believed they were in the top 30% of safe drivers. The reality suggested a quite different picture.

In 1987, John Cannell did a study that reported the statistically impossible finding that all states claimed average student test scores above the national norm.

One College Board survey asked 829,000 high school seniors to rate themselves in a number of ways. When asked to rate their own ability to "get along with others," a statistically insignificant number – less than 1% – rated themselves as below average. Further, 60% rated themselves in the top 10% and 25% rated themselves in the top 1%.

How about you?

How accurate are self-evaluations?

SPEED OF OPPORTUNITY

The key difference between ordinary and extraordinary players is that the great ones are always thinking one, two or three plays ahead.
PAT RILEY
The Winner Within

We've established that the quality of your results is directly related to the quality of your evaluations. We know that the quality of your evaluations is linked to the quality of your questions. Now we are adding another factor – the need for speed.

Your results are affected by the speed with which you can complete the evaluation and take action. *Why is speed important?*

As discussed earlier, agility and speed of response are critical to the success of organizations and individuals. We have access to greater and greater amounts of information coming at us faster and faster as technology advances.

In order to survive, we must be able to quickly and effectively sort through the input (both external and internal) and distinguish the important from the unimportant, and the relevant from the irrelevant data.

Paul Rogers and Marcia Blenko, writing in *The Harvard Business Review*, noted that:

> **Making good decisions and making them happen quickly are the hallmarks of high-performing organizations.**

Their study of top executives at 350 global companies found that what set top performers apart is the quality, speed and execution of their decision making.

They also found that successful decision-driven organizations tend to follow a few clear principles:

- Some decisions matter more than others.
- The decisions that are crucial to building value in the business are the ones that matter most.
- Action is the goal.
- Good decision making doesn't end with a decision; it ends with implementation.
- Ambiguity is the enemy.
- Clear accountability is essential.

- Speed and adaptability are crucial.

- A company that makes good decisions quickly has a higher metabolism which allows it to act on opportunities and overcome obstacles.

- Practice beats preaching.

- Involve the people who will live with the new decision roles in designing them.

Success in business depends on our ability to scan the landscape for opportunities and dangers. **We need to be able to anticipate potential problems and take action, rather than waiting and reacting to them.**

Consider Wayne Gretzky. Gretzky scored more points than anyone in the history of the National Hockey League.

What made him so effective?

Was it because he's the biggest, strongest, or fastest player in the league? By his own admission, the answer to all three of these questions is no. Yet he was consistently the #1 scorer in the league.

When asked what made him so effective, his response was that while most players skated to where the puck was, he tended to skate to *where the puck was going*. At any moment in time, his ability to anticipate – to *evaluate* the velocity of the puck, its direction, the strategies and momentum of the players around him – allowed him to place himself in the best position for scoring.

How can you increase the quality and speed of your daily decisions?

RESULTS-DRIVEN LEADERS

The best way for results-driven leaders to improve their evaluations is to ensure they're providing adequate support for individuals and their decision-making. *Why?* Because the effectiveness of an organization's evaluation is merely the sum of the individual evaluations being made every minute of every day.

Gary Neilson and Bruce Pasternack, authors of *Results*, help to prove this point:

> *An organization's overall performance is simply the sum total of all the actions and decisions that people inside it take every day. At some fundamental level, everyone is constantly making decisions and managing trade-offs, whether it's how to price a customer quote, which engineering projects to fund given a limited budget, or what phone calls or e-mails to return first. These are not big, boardroom issues; they are the mundane action items that incrementally drive the business forward. How well and how efficiently individuals in a firm make these decisions largely determines the organization's success in the marketplace.*[14]

For these reasons, **a leader must ensure it is hiring and retaining the type of talent that can consistently make effective evaluations.** Consider the impact an effective evaluation had on this leader and company:

In 1981 a new airline was struggling. It was getting an inordinate number of complaints about many of its flight attendants. The firm hired a consultant to figure out the solution. The consultant was Rodger Bailey, who had just completed a two-year project of developing the internal mentoring program for IBM.

Bailey applied the same organizational evaluations to this new challenge. He discovered that most of the flight attendants were not focused on the passengers as people. Passengers were seen as elements of the industry, like luggage or cargo. Bailey also discovered that the flight attendants who did perceive passengers as people were rated very high by the passengers. So he taught the human resources department how to make more effective evaluations to attract and hire talent with this ability.

Did it work? The airline was Southwest, unquestionably one of the most successful airlines in aviation history. One of the reasons for that success is that Southwest flight attendants are extremely personable and natu-

---

15. *Results: Keep What's Good, Fix What's Wrong, and Unlock Great Performance* by Gary L. Neilson, Bruce A. Pasternack

rally focused on the passengers. Bailey had discovered a highly effective way to evaluate the needs of Southwest airlines and close the results gap.

What are the key areas for your organization to evaluate?

MIND YOUR BUSINESS

*Thinking is the hardest work there is, which is
probably why so few engage in it.*
HENRY FORD

Let's take a few minutes to understand the process of evaluating. **Top performing individuals and organizations are consistently evaluating the present and preparing for the future.** The process of evaluating involves the identification of key external events (Outlook – what I observe) and the interpretation of those events (Inlook – what it means to me).

EVALUATIONS = OUTLOOK + INLOOK

Consider the fact that organizations look out for emerging trends, global events and industry issues. Then they look inward to interpret or translate these changes into potential pain or gain for the organization. It is this interpretation that forms the "Inlook."

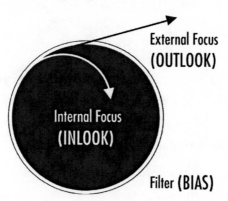

See the process of an evaluation? It encapsulates your outward observations and your inward interpretations.

Individuals do the same thing. They look externally to identify business issues, and then determine how these issues might impact them or their job.

A gap often exists at both the organizational and individual levels.

Organizations are usually competent at identifying and interpreting the impact of events and situations on the business. However, they typically don't look at how those events and situations will affect the individuals in their organizations.

Similarly, individuals are good at identifying business issues and how those things might affect their jobs or them personally. However, most have a very limited view and fail to interpret market trends appropriately.

To achieve superior results, organizations must have an Inlook which accommodates the individual. To be Top Performers, individuals must have an outlook which accommodates business-related events and situations.

THE FILTER FACTOR?

Truth like football – receive many kicks before reaching goal.
CHARLIE CHAN

It is essential that you understand the filters or biases that affect your evaluations. We all have a certain way of looking at things that affect our focus and clarity. We have beliefs about how things are or how they're supposed to be. We make assumptions that may or may not be valid.

We see this often in sales situations. The seller has certain assumptions about clients. For example:

- They're in this industry so they must be ...

- They'll want ...

- They'll be motivated by ...

- They dislike ...

Assumptions are a natural part of our mental work. An assumption is a generalization. Most companies are client-centric, most doors open in the same way, sharp objects can hurt you. If we didn't generalize, we would not be able to see patterns in life. So generalizing can be useful, but your assumptions must be tested.

How do you test assumptions?

Simple. Ask questions. For example:

- Is this really true?

- How do I know it's true?

- What evidence do I have that it's true?

- Is it always true? Sometimes true?

- What could be assumed instead?

- How is this assumption serving me?

- Do I need to adjust my thinking?

So, clean your mental filters and test your assumptions to ensure that your filters are not factors in accurately interpreting situations.

THE MASTER KEYS

Here are the master keys to making superior evaluations:

1. Suspending judgment

2. Avoiding oversimplifications

3. Exploring underlying beliefs, emotions, feelings

4. Clarifying issues, conclusions, beliefs

5. Developing criteria for evaluation: clarifying values and standards

6. Evaluating the credibility of sources of information

7. Questioning deeply: raising and pursuing root or significant questions

8. Analyzing or evaluating arguments, interpretations, beliefs, or theories

9. Generating or assessing solutions

10. Listening critically

11. Asking clarifying questions

12. Comparing and contrasting

13. Distinguishing relevant from irrelevant facts

14. Exploring implications and consequences

THE TOP VS. AVERAGE PERFORMERS

Average is being at the Top of the bottom!
MAMA

What separates Top Performers from those who struggle?

Top Performers consistently evaluate and refine their standards, talents, evaluations, preparation, action and results. Average Performers are satisfied with current standards, talents, evaluations, preparation, actions and results.

Top Performers are disciplined evaluators and they ask consistent questions. They evaluate from the bottom up (start with Self), while Average Performers evaluate from the top down.

Top Performers ask possibility questions and test assumptions. They regularly clean their mental filters so that they can evaluate situations accurately. Average Performers tend to ask problem questions and base decisions on assumptions which may or may not be valid.

Here's a summary:

Top Performers	Average Performers
Keep Score Daily	Keep Score Occasionally
Bottom-up Evaluations	Top-down Evaluations
Focused on the Future	Satisfied with the Present
See the Possibilities	See the Problems
Test Assumptions	Regret Assumptions

Here are the key action steps of this chapter:

1. Identify and Close Your Results Gap.

Start by evaluating your current actual state vs. your desired future state. *What specific actions can you take in the next 30 days to close the gap?*

2. Step Up Your Decision-making.

Make the invisible visible. Understand the connection between your questions, your actions and your results.

3. Improve the Quality of Your Questions.

Identify your top three daily questions and evaluate them. *Are they serving or sabotaging you?*

4. Evaluate Yourself.

Play back the tapes of your performance each day and make mid-course corrections to improve your results.

5. Expand Your Thinking.

Accurately evaluate the changing marketplace and effectively interpret how these changes will impact the individual and organization. Test your assumptions and distinguish facts from opinions.

Step Four

PROPER PREPARATION

They had the Roman Appetite to Win,
but they lacked the Spartan Discipline to Prepare!
NFL FILMS

Are you properly prepared to achieve superior results?

Becoming a world-class professional requires the same type of preparation that other top performers invest in. Athletes, doctors, entrepreneurs – you name the profession. The best in these professions prepare themselves every day to reach the top and stay there. **The daily investment they make is self-preparation**, the constant and never-ending process of preparing and improving oneself to achieve superior results.

Preparation is driven by an enlightened self-interest. It's about being a student of results. It's about gathering the necessary know-how through practicing, executing and learning to create the best results in business and life.

In most of us there is a results gap (the distance between our actual and potential results) **that represents the greatest opportunity for increased profit for the individual and organization.** The closing of your results gap is based on greater preparation and personal development.

> **PREPARATION IS:**
> - A process, not a single event.
> - Self-development.
> - Anticipating the future.

PERSONAL PREPARATION

*What happens to a man is less significant than
what happens within him.*
LOUIS L. MANN

With your permission, I'd like to share another sliver of my personal story with you, because it illustrates how proper preparation can help you turn obstacles into opportunities.

Several months after being denied a sales position with Huthwaite, one of their employees happened to see me make a brief presentation at a social event. He was impressed and encouraged me to immediately apply as a sales trainer at Huthwaite.

But I was reluctant to apply. *Why?* Well, I was unclear about why I hadn't been awarded the sales position months earlier. *Did I lack the talent? Was the organization biased? Or were the other candidates just a better fit?* After more introspection, I decided to STEP UP and pursue this new opportunity to be a member of one of the most highly regarded organizations in the sales training community.

Huthwaite requested I fly to their corporate headquarters and showcase my talents. *Have you seen the showcase on American Idol?* That's exactly what it was like. They gave me a few minutes to do my thing. *And what happened?* **This time, I got the job!** I was invited to become a member of their elite faculty delivering their sales seminars across the globe. *What was the difference?* A little bit of luck and lots of preparation!

There is no excellency without difficulty.
OVID

Initially, I was given the "low visibility" programs like engagements in Iowa with four participants. *Do you get the picture?* **So, I kept preparing, getting feedback and stepping up.** *And then?* Huthwaite began entrusting me with their "high visibility" clients such as Google, IBM and UPS. In 2005, I was voted MVP (Most Valuable Presenter) within their network. Then, Huthwaite made a special request for me to coach their new sales consultants and teach them how to be more effective.

Think about that for a moment. Huthwaite had **rejected** my attempts to become one of their new sales consultants. Yet, just three years later, they invited me to lead the sales training for all their new sales consultants. *How's that for a reversal in results?* And the key to this reversal in results was proper preparation. You see, obstacles are just stepping stones on the road to superior results and **preparation is the keystone** on that path.

You'll never guess what happened to me next. You can turn to the next chapter later to find out. For now, let's return to our larger discussion about proper preparation.

ACHIEVING TIP TOP RESULTS

To Improve Performance, Think On Paper
DANIEL GRISSOM

Imagine that it's Monday morning. It's the start of your new business week. *Typically, do you have a written list of your goals for the day?* Okay, let's say it's the end of the business day. You've made a couple of key sales call. *Typically, do you send the client a follow-up email summarizing the call outcomes?* Okay, one last time. It's the middle of the month and you're behind on your sales plan. *Typically, can you look into your sales journal to review your actions?*

If your answer was "No" to the majority of these questions, then its likely that you are not achieving **TIP TOP** results. It's an acronym, which stand for **To Improve Performance Think on Paper**. There are many methods for thinking on paper, but there is just one outcome – superior results!

Think about it. When you go grocery shopping without a written list, *what happens?* When you try to solve a complex math problem in your head, *what happens?* Or when you go to worship, but fail to take notes during the sermon, *what happens?* The answer is errors in execution. *Why?* **It's because failing to think on paper puts your results at risk of being forgotten.**

But, we know that. We know that planning on paper improves per-formance. *So, if we know what to do, then why don't we do what we know?* The answer is the lack of self-discipline. *What is self-discipline?* **It's the time elapsed between a good thought and action.** It's the bridge between goals and results. It's the antithesis of procrastination. *What is procrasti-nation?* **It's knowing what to do, but not doing what you know.**

———

The current price of excellence is self discipline, but the future cost of procrastination is regret!
MAMA

You see, when you "put it on paper", you activate your super-conscious mind and it works to achieve your desired result. Also, once activated, it **will hold you personally accountable for the results you have recorded**. But when you don't write it down, you de-activate this superpower and sidestep personal accountability.

My experience and field observation reveals that top performers think on paper. They write down their call objective and plan a few effective questions to use during the call. They send agendas in advance of the call. They email a summary of the call outcomes to the client after the call. *Should you develop these habits?*

A goal without a plan is a daydream.
NATHANIEL BRANDEN

In summary, **proper preparation prevents poor performance**. And this begins with thinking on paper and self discipline. So, if you want better results, then you've got to STEP UP and get into **TIP TOP** shape.

PRE-CALL PLANNING

You've got to begin asking hard questions in a soft way.
WILLIAM T. BROOKS

As we established in the Standards Chapter, the purpose of a sales call is to engage the client in a business dialogue and help them to think, act and win. And, one of our primary tools for achieving this result is a question. Think about it. During any business dialogue, **you have two communication tools of influence – a statement and a question.**

And of course, a statement sets forth facts, observations, or opinions. In other words, it supplies information. A question, on the other hand, draws out this same information. The word question is derived from the word quest, which is a search or pursuit undertaken to discover something of value.

So, **statements push and questions pull**. Yet, when it comes to influence, research shows that questions are often more powerful than statements. Pull is stronger than push. *Why's that?* It's because statements invite the client to consider your thoughts, which is good. But in contrast, questions invite the client to consider their own thoughts, which is best. Questions lead to self-discovery. Questions invite the client to follow the advice of their #1 coach – themselves.

Compelling questions stimulate thinking and provoke client insight and action. **The quality of your call is commensurate with the quality of the questions you ask on the call.** So, let's talk about how you can best plan and organize your questions prior to making a sales call.

First, **the basis for any business dialogue is pain and gain**. That's right. It's about avoiding pain or achieving gain in business. Pain based questions ask about the client's business problems, challenges, difficulties and dissatisfactions. Gain based questions ask about the client's business goals, initiatives, projects and desired outcomes. You want to be prepared to ask both type of questions on the sales call because some clients response more to pain than gain and vice-versa.

Second, **the basis ofor any business dialogus is current and future state**. Current state questions invite the client to think about their current condition. Future state questions invite the client to think about their future condition. The difference between their current state and future state is the results gap. This gap represents the greatest potential for you and your organization to create client value and results. Here's a small sample of effective questions that you can plan to help you achieve the right results on your next sales call:

Investigating Pain and Gain (Present State)

- What are your top 3 challenges you'd like to solve within the next 12 months?

- What are the top 3 goals you'd like to achieve in the next 12 months?

- What are the key changes in your business over the last 12 months?

- What's most important to you about this decision?

- What is the ideal outcome you'd like to achieve?

Developing Pain and Gain (Future State)

- What are the risks of not changing your behavior?

- If this problem worsens, what would happen?

- Could this solution help you achieve your goals?

- What would solving this problem mean to you personally?

- If your competitor solves this problem before you do, what could that mean?

If you'd like a complete list of questions that you can use on your next sales call, then drop me an email at **daniel@phdinresults.com** and I'll send you the list.

THE RESULTS CYCLE

Take a look at the previous visual. It illustrates a process that can improve your performance and results. The process begins with preparing a plan, then working your plan and reviewing your plan. **This is the results cycle.** Most salespeople invest their time in taking action. This is the good news. The bad news is taking action without pre-call planning and post-call review reduces the quality of each call while concurrently reducing client value and sales results.

Sadly, the misuse of the results cycle rings true in personal life, too. Think about how most of us behave when we decide to attend church. We "take action" and go to the Sunday service. But, *do we prepare before going to service by reading a few scriptures in advance? Do we examine our notes after the sermon and digest the lessons learned?* Let me ask you a better question. *How would our results improve if we did?*

No, most of us don't use the results cycle effectively in sales or leadership. But you can change that by stepping up and using the results cycle.

PREPARE TO WIN

The secret to success in life is for a man to be ready for his time when it comes.
BENJAMIN DISRAELI

The quality and quantity of your preparation should be calibrated with the importance of the goal and the difficulty of achieving it. Take a look at the visual above.

This simple tool gives you a graphic representation of the planning effort required to achieve the best results. A goal that is both difficult and important to achieve will require major planning like making a sales call on a new high potential account. A goal that is easy to accomplish, but still important, will require moderate planning like making a sales call on a familiar client with moderate potential.

A goal that is more difficult than important will require a plan to manage or support it like completing paperwork while trying to make more sales calls. Finally, a goal that is easy to accomplish, but marginally important will require only minor planning. An example would be mapping out your day to ensure you have time to go to refuel your car so you can make more sales calls.

How much is the lack of planning costing you?

Consider this. **If a seller leaves $50,000 per year on the table due to the lack of planning, that's $1 million over 10 years of opportunity cost for the individual.** If two sellers do the same, that's $100K per year and $10 million for 10 years of opportunity cost for the organization! Ensure you're ready to achieve the best results via proper preparation and planning.

SLOW DOWN TO SPEED UP

*We curse the effect (lack of results), but we nourish the cause
(lack of proper planning).*
DANIEL GRISSOM

Most of us know that preparation is key. Sure, we may know what to do, but *do we consistently do what we know?* Too often we fail to prepare and I believe there are three primary reasons for this:

1. We don't know how to plan.

2. We don't make the time to plan.

3. We lack the discipline to plan.

Average performers quickly "jump into action" while top performers slow down to plan which speeds up their results. For example, instead of making six sales calls that are B+ in quality, top performers slow down and make four sales calls that are A+ in quality. They slow down and invest the proper amount of time and resources to ensure they are adequately prepared before the call, then invest the time to review the call to distill the "lessons learned" and use these insights to ready themselves for the next call.

In summary, the future of business involves slowing down. **You must slow down to speed up.** Stop for a second and consider that thought. In businesses today, most professionals see a problem and immediately start throwing solutions at it. **Step back. Slow down and plan.**

You should consider possible solutions before throwing money at it or wasting time with poor execution. By slowing down and planning, you prepare for an excellent result. Before calling a business contact, step back and learn about their position, company, and desired results. By helping your clients achieve their results, you in turn will also achieve your own. Stop wasting time with ill-conceived plans and prepare to march forward with a well-conceived plan.

LESSONS FROM THE LUMBERJACKS

Be patiently aggressive.
WINSTON CHURCHILL

Have you ever seen a Lumberjack contest on television?

It's a contest between two lumberjacks to determine who can cut the most wood in a targeted period of time.

Let me share a story with you that further illustrates the importance of slowing down to speed up.

There was a major lumberjack contest. One of the lumberjacks was a big burly looking guy and his competitor was a kind, small skinny looking guy. They both hacked with an axe for eight straight hours to determine who was the strongest.

Each hour the skinny guy stopped, looked at his watch, and walked off the stage to take a 10-minute break. Then he came back and started chopping again. An hour later he stopped again, looked at his watch and walked off stage for another 10-minute break.

At the end of this eight-hour contest, the smaller guy cut more wood and won the competition! The big burly guy was confused and embarrassed. He greeted the winner and said, "Congratulations, but *how did you beat me when you were taking all of those breaks?*"

The winner said, "I wasn't taking a break at all. I was taking the time to sharpen my axe because when I slow down I go faster."

This story is a great business metaphor because all of us know that we need to take time to sharpen our axe or sales and leadership skills. **It's about working smarter, not working harder. It's about slowing down to prepare in order to speed up results!**

ACTION PLANS

Everyone's preparation is either a warning or an example.
Which will yours be?
DANIEL GRISSOM

Plan for Results

```
        A
ACTIONS |
        |  ┌──────────┬──────────┐
        |  │          │          │
        |  │ GAMBLER  │ ACHIEVER │
        |  │          │          │
        |  ├──────────┼──────────┤
        |  │          │          │
        |  │ SPECTATOR│  TALKER  │
        |  │          │          │
        |  └──────────┴──────────┘
        |─────────────────────────────▶
          WEAK    PLANS    STRONG
```

See the visual above. It illustrates that some sellers are quick to take action, but they "Gamble" on their results because of their lack of preparation. Some sellers prepare well and "Talk" a good game, but fail to act. And of course, there are those sellers that do neither and are mere "Spectators."

However, "Achiever" performers are different. They slow down to plan, then take strategic action. This is the combination of behaviors that produces the best results.

Where would you plot yourself?

Are your results a warning or an example?

You should plan your Day the Night before.

THE POWER OF PLANNING

He who does not look ahead will remain behind.
CHINESE PROVERB

What's the #1 factor that separates top performers from average performers?

According to research, by Dr. Peter Gollwitzer, Professor of Psychology at New York University, the answer is Superior Preparation!

Dr. Gollwitzer conducted several studies that demonstrate the benefits of making specific plans that outline when, where, and how to perform an action. Dr. Gollwitzer argues that plans allow people to more easily remember specifically what to do.

Here are the payoffs:

First, they don't waste time trying to recall what it is they are going to do. They've already made the commitment and decided what to do, and in what situation, beforehand. When put to the test, they have little trouble following that plan.

Second, people act more quickly when they have a plan to follow.

Third, when people have a plan, they can more easily ignore interruptions and distractions. They are able to more easily focus on the task at hand. In short, proper preparation empowers you to control your destiny and improve results.[16]

Think about golf as an analogy. Every hole in golf is assigned a minimum standard called "par." That stands for the "average performance results." So shooting par is being average. Not bad, but of course you can't become a successful golfer (or anything) by merely shooting par.

How do the best golfers ensure they consistently perform above par?

They prepare!

---

16. *Psychology of Action: Linking Cognition and Motivation to Behavior* by Gollwitzer, Peter M.

How do they prepare?

They practice!

Anyone who is a Master at any endeavor understands that practice improves performance. Master golfers have learned to expect a significant return on their investment – the investment of their preparation time. They know the difference between winning and losing is often only one or two strokes. And the lack of practice can easily cost you one or two strokes. This is true in sales and leadesrhip as well.

You don't need to beat your competition by 10 strokes. You just need to win by one or two strokes. **Small improvements can produce big results.**

You don't win in the game. You win in the preparation.

SET DEMANDING GOALS

The best way to predict the future is to create it.
PETER DRUCKER

In order to produce superior results, you must first decide what you want. Create a crystallized mental picture of it. *What do superior results for you look like?* Then write it, draw it, or find photos of it.

The most effective consultants, coaches and mentors help their clients identify goals. What they discover is that often the clients do not have a clear sense of what they want to achieve. For example, many professionals and business owners say their goal is to improve their success. However, they can't describe what "success" looks like.

In such situations, the following process is invaluable and is arguably the most powerful process on the planet for defining goals and getting results! It is a process borrowed from the world's great psychotherapists. **What you get when you follow these steps is called a "Well-Formed Outcome."** When the goal is important to you, and you want to make sure you achieve it, simply answer these questions:

What do you want to achieve?

This seemingly simple question is where many people create failure. The question looks for two things – possibility and direction.

Possibility. Some goals are impossible to achieve. *Ever watch the Miss America contest? What do you hear every year as the number one goal? "Achieve world peace!" Now, is that doable by those lovely and talented young women within the next year?* Of course not. That's an example of a goal that is impossible to achieve because it is too big. A better answer might be, "Feed 300 needy children every week for the next year."

Direction. Some roads lead to success, and some lead away from it. Those that lead away are headed in the wrong direction. To a Roman optimist, all roads led to Rome. The point is, unless you state your goal or outcome in positive language, you're heading in the wrong direction. For example, if you're in sales, you might say, "I want to grow the size of my territory by 10 percent." You would not say, "I want to avoid market stagnation." A goal stated in the positive allows you to focus on opportunities to make it happen. A goal stated in the negative interrupts your thoughts and stops you in your tracks.

Is this a goal you can achieve on your own?

Who's in charge? Is the outcome of your goal under your control or influence? Your goal must be something that is within your control. For example, you would say, "I want to exceed my quota and earn my bonus. You wouldn't say, "I want my boss to give me a bigger bonus."

If your goal is to write a book, but you can't type, you might find that the goal is impossible. In that situation, a better goal would be to complete a class in typing.

What are the advantages and disadvantages of achieving this goal?

This is known as an "ecology check." It is the question that causes many people to modify their goal or scrap it altogether when they realize that in order to achieve the goal, they will have to give up something else that is more important.

If you want to become the top salesperson in your firm, it is likely to require you to be out of town every week. That could destroy your family. *Which one is more important to you?* If you want to write a book, and you complete the typing class, you will then be put to the test – can you write prose that people want to read? If you doubt your creativity, you might value the dream more than the reality.

This question forces you to make some tough decisions. Dick Vermeil was the coach of the Kansas City Chiefs. He was caught between his love for the game and his love for his family. In order to achieve his goal of winning the Super Bowl, he would have to sacrifice his family, and he was not prepared to do that. Coach Vermeil resigned from the Chiefs to spend time with his family.

On a scale of 1 to 10, how important is it for you to achieve this goal?

This question determines your motivation for achieving the goal. It could be a goal that satisfies every criteria, but one that you are not passionate about. If so, you're not apt to succeed at it. The TV show *American Idol* exposes many people who would like to become pop stars, but they don't have enough desire to take voice lessons. It also exposes other people who would pay any price to win.

What is important to you about achieving this goal?

This question looks at your values in the context of that goal. Every goal has associated values. If you find that you can't answer the question, then the goal probably doesn't fit easily within your values. The goals that are most easily achieved are those that are perfectly in sync with your values.

Where does this goal take you next?

This question puts your success into perspective of a bigger goal and helps define the direction for your life or career. The most successful goals are next steps in a process of greater achievement. Achieving each goal takes you one step closer to the achievement of a much larger goal. When you look back at your goals over a five- or 10-year period, *did you achieve more and more each year?*

Many people discover that they achieve the same goals over and over. That's because the goal is not part of a process of improvement. For example, lose 20 pounds – then what? Most people find that they then gain those pounds right back. Get a big client – *then what?*

If you haven't written it down, then you haven't thought it through!

MENTAL READINESS

The mind is the limit. As long as the mind can envision the fact that you can do something, you can do it – as long as you really believe 100 percent.
ARNOLD SCHWARZENEGGER

Jack Nicklaus (world-renown champion golfer) said, "I never hit a golf shot without having a sharp picture of it in my head. First, **I see where I want the ball to finish.** Then I see it going there; its trajectory and landing. The next scene shows me making the swing that will turn the previous images into reality."

Nicklaus is seeing a little mental movie of his successful shot. He literally steps out of actual play and into the Theater of the Mind to watch the movie. Then he steps back out to experience the déjà vu effect. In an article in *Golf Magazine (July 2000)*, Nicklaus said, "the more deeply you ingrain what I like to call my going-to-the-movies discipline, the more effective you will become at hitting shots you want to hit."

Research Quarterly reported an experiment on the effects of mental practice on improving skill in sinking basketball free throws. One group of students practiced throwing the ball every day for 20 days, and was scored on the first and last days.

A second group was scored on the first and last days too, but it did no practice in between.

A third group was scored on the first day, and then invested 20 minutes a day, imagining that they were throwing the ball at the goal. When they missed they would imagine that they corrected their aim accordingly.

The first group, which actually practiced 20 minutes every day, improved scoring by 24%. The second group, which had no practice, showed no improvement. The third group, which practiced only in their imagination, improved scoring by 23%!

This particular experiment has been widely reported, referenced and repeated many times at various universities over the years. While scientifically valid, the research can't really give you a fool-proof formula for hitting 100% of your free throws. If it did Shaquille O'Neal's dilemma would be over! **The use of visualization is an effective applied science, a proven and practical means of improving results.**[17]

What's your next big sales call or leadership meeting?

Are you mentally prepared?

17. *Psycho Cybernetics 2000* by Bobbe Sommer with Mark Falstein. Prentice-Hall, 1993

BUILDING MENTAL MUSCLES

———•———

Fortune favors the prepared mind.
LOUIS PASTEUR

Research in neurology provides conclusive evidence that practice does indeed produce superior results. Our brains are constantly changing throughout our lives. Connections between neurons are strengthened or weakened as we learn new skills and acquire new memories. These circuitry changes, called "brain plasticity," optimize the brain's function to meet each individual's needs.

Let's say I decide one day that I want to improve my golf swing, become a better dancer or learn to identify my client's communication style. Once that decision is made, my brain is happy to oblige and begin rewiring its circuits to allow those changes (allow plasticity). However, it requires repetition and time (about 21 days) to firmly establish the plasticity and make the change permanent.

We know from studies of learning that plasticity depends on repetition and attention. If I intently practice bird call identification, for example, the part of my brain that responds to these sounds would increase, making it easier for me to distinguish the subtle differences between them. However, if I simply heard the sounds over and over without focusing on them, there would be no change in my brain and I would learn nothing. Focused attention stimulates release of neurotransmitters that encourage plasticity and learning. Without this mechanism to regulate plasticity, our neurons would try to learn every detail about common, but useless stimuli like air conditioner sounds for example.

David Weiner, author of *Reality Check: What Your Mind Knows But Isn't Telling You*, references research that shows there are two important reasons why practice makes perfect. The first is that when you practice anything – be it a sales presentation or Beethoven's "Moonlight" sonata

– you essentially carve an efficient path for it in your brain. However, without practice, your brain can take any of tens or hundreds of paths to reach its final destination.

The bottom line is practice reduces the number of potential pathways. By repeating your presentation again and again, you'll start using only about eight to ten pathways. Weiner says, "The brain will know what you want it to do, so you'll become more precise."

The delivery of a presentation is a single act that is repeated. The playing of a piece of music is a single act that is repeated. *What if you want to master something that is seemingly random?* Staying with our theme, let's say you want to be able to connect with anyone, any of the different personality types, and appeal to any set of values. The possible combinations are vast. But simply putting yourself in enough situations would allow complex plasticity to take shape.

This is the same formula that allows great improvisational musicians to endlessly create fresh, new combinations. Listening to artists like James Brown, Louis Armstrong and Charlie Parker, you discover that the number of ideas and the speed at which they come is mind-boggling. Still, it is all made possible through practice. Lots of practice at doing the same thing in different ways establishes exponentially more neuro pathways.

TIME MANAGEMENT TIPS

In preparing for battle I have always found that plans
are useless, but planning is indispensable.
DWIGHT EISENHOWER
U.S. General and President

Another tool you can use for planning and time management is the four-quadrant Strategic and Tactical chart. I call this the STIC chart

(Strategic-Tactical-Important-Critical). Think about what you have in front of you and organize it into these four buckets:

Strategic and Critical – Key to the long-term success of your business and needs to be done immediately

Strategic and Important – Important to the long-term success of your business, but does not necessarily need to be done immediately

Tactical and Critical – Important and needs to be done right away

Tactical and Important – Important but does not necessarily need to be done right away

If you have items on your list that don't meet any of these criteria, then you need to ask yourself why you're doing them. *Should they even be on your list?*

Here's an example STIC chart:

Strategically Critical	Tactically Critical
1. Complete negotiations with alliance partners and sign contract 2. Hire assistant 3. Complete background research on new prospect and prepare for meeting	1. Complete brochure and send to the printer 2. File tax returns by the 15th 3. Consolidate databases before February mailing 4. Contact all new prospects by April 1
Strategically Important	Tactically Important
1. Collect feedback from clients 2. Re-engineer client service processes 3. Upgrade technology platform	1. Update website with new product information 2. Complete expense report 3. Order office supplies

THE CHALLENGE OF CHANGE

*Change is the law of life. And those who look only to
the past or present are certain to miss the future.*
JOHN F. KENNEDY
35th President of the United States

Preparation and anticipation work hand in hand to produce superior results. The flip side is also relevant – without these two components, failure is a very real possibility.

Failure is generally the result of not accurately anticipating the future. This is true both at an individual level and at an organization level. Human psychology is to assume things will remain the same when in fact they never do. Change is inevitable, especially at this time in history, and highly effective people are those who prepare for the change.

A big part of being prepared is learning to anticipate the future. The antithesis of anticipation is reaction, and reaction sounds like this, "I'll deal with it when it comes." It often sounds like, "Oops!" Suffice it to say, you want to experience the power of preparation, not the pain of reaction. **You must anticipate change versus being struck by it.**

A proactive seller or leader anticipates and is constantly "out there" interacting with the environment, looking for signals and signs of change and preparing themselves to capitalize.

Perhaps we should call anticipating the gift of foresight. After all, it is like seeing into the future. Once you learn how to prepare for the changes and anticipate the trends in the marketplace, you are in a position to anticipate opportunities and get there before your competitors. Likewise, you can anticipate a problem and solve it before it happens. This will provide you with a huge competitive advantage.

Focusing on your client's or prospect's current needs is no longer enough. Anticipating their needs before they demand it is a great way to enhance your results.

Why? John Narver of the University of Washington Business School describes it this way, "Customers' expressed needs and benefits can be known readily by all competitors – a situation that leads typically to competitors offering the same benefits to a given set of customers and then having to engage in aggressive price competition in the attempt to create superior value for the subject customers."[18]

In brief, knowledge of the client's "expressed" current needs is readily available to anyone, and it's easy for your competitors to propose the same solutions. However, **if you can anticipate the client's needs before he does, you will position yourself to be the solution of the future. You will leap frog over the competition.**

S.E.E. THE FUTURE

Anticipate change and embrace it; change can affect the entire picture. Recognize new developments that you can capitalize on, profit from and use to open new doors.
DONALD TRUMP

How can you know what customers will want even before they see it themselves? How can you anticipate future problems and help customers avoid pain and achieve gain? Simple. Employ the S.E.E. method to see or anticipate the future.

S.E.E. is the process of **S**.tudying the market (segment, industry or niche) of your prospect to anticipate the **E**.ffects on business and **E**.ffects

18. *Successful Development of New Products Requires Anticipating Customers Needs*, UWnews.org, October 2004

MARKET

BUSINESS

PERSONAL

personally. It's a line of sight that leads to insight into your client's mindset.

First, you must S.tudy the news reports and newspapers to identify the current and urgent trends or changes that are taking place in your client's market. **It's intelligence gathering that requires you to look for really good news or really bad news.** I'm not just talking about the obvious trends and changes. Look for those that are strategically insightful, but perhaps not detected by the client's radar. This will prepare you to intrigue your prospect with such comments as: "*Are you aware that the emerging trends in your market could be eroding your bottom line?* I've observed this with my other key clients. *Would you be interested in meeting to discuss the implications on your organization?*"

Second, your must translate the E.ffects these market trends will have on your clients' business. Here's what I mean. Market trends trickle down and Effect the business (your client). These effects cause new pain or gain for the client's business. **You must understand and anticipate this pain or gain before your competition.**

Finally, you must anticipate the effects these business trends are having on the client personally. Clients take action not just because it's the right thing to do for the business, but because of how it personally affects them or their careers as well.

SUMMARY

You've studied the industry and its current trends. You have translated its Effects on business. You anticipated how these business impacts are affecting the individual. Now you can more accurately understand the present and anticipate the future. **You can S.E.E.**

THE TOP VS. AVERAGE PERFORMERS

———————

Average is being at the Top of the bottom!
MAMA

What separates Top Performers from those who struggle?

Top Performers have a mental picture of the end results they want to achieve. They also make them explicit by writing the goals and the steps for achieving them on paper. Average Performers, on the other hand, often come up with wonderful ideas, but rather than putting them down on paper, they keep their ideas in their head.

Top Performers slow down to speed up, while Average Performers speed up to slow down.

Top Performers watch developments and trends as their way to prevent problems before they occur. Average Performers focus on solving problems after they occur.

Top Performers anticipate. They are forward-looking and forward-thinking. Average Performers tend to be reactive, only dealing with what's immediately in front of them.

Here's a summary:

Top Performers	Average Performers
Prepare on Paper	Prepare in Their Head
Long-term Thinking	Short-term Thinking
Slow Down to Speed Up	Speed Up and Slow Down
Plan Outcomes	Plan Activities
Anticipate	React

THE KEY ACTION STEPS

Proper Preparation

Here are the key action steps of this chapter:

1. **Learn to Think on Paper.**

   Get your plans out of your head and get them on paper. Writing increases clarity and commitment.

2. **Be Clear and Specific About Your Goals.**

   Define the results you want to achieve and how you will achieve them. Chart your progress and be prepared to adjust your plans as things around you change.

3. **Be a Student of Anticipation.**

   Identify potential scenarios for how industry changes might impact your customers. Anticipate problems and opportunities before your clients do and be prepared to help them respond effectively.

4. **Read Every Day.**

   Not reports, but personal growth materials because business growth seldom exceeds personal growth.

5. **Work Harder on Yourself Than You Do on Your Job.**

   If you work hard on your job, you'll make a living. If you work harder on yourself, you can make a fortune.

Step Five

UNLEASH YOUR POTENTIAL

You can always better your best!
MAMA

Do Your Actions match Your Potential? If not, why not?

Through the last four chapters, we've talked about Standards, Talents, Evaluations and Preparation. Although these are all key components of the results model, they aren't worth much without the final component – Action and Execution!

These earlier four components form the base or platform from which you take action or Unleash Your Potential. They ensure you take the right actions, specifically the one that will empower you to achieve superior results. **Action is often the difference between "good" and "great" results!**

Let me ask you a question, *what do you think the potential is for any human being?* Let me ask you another question, *Are the results in most people's lives consistent with their real potential? Why not?* I think it's because most people do not live up to their potential in business. You must become one of the few who do.

> **UNLEASHING POTENTIAL IS:**
>
> - Taking consistent action to close your results gap.
> - The bridge between potential and results.
> - The process of implementing.

PERSONAL POWER

Daniel is a unique blend of a business thinker and personal motivator. He helped our organization. I believe he can help you too.
TIM ARMSTRONG
President, Advertising & Commerce, Google

With your permission, I'd like to share another sliver of my personal story. It illustrates how you can **advance from mediocrity to mastery** when you STEP UP and unleash your potential. Earlier this year, I was given a unique opportunity. It was the ultimate professional challenge. The choices were clear. Either I had to step up or back down from it.

I was invited to help Huthwaite work with a highly prized client. The prized client was one of the new corporate giants – Google! I was one member of a select faculty, six leaders who were asked to deliver sales strategy sessions to hundreds of young business executives at Google. These were sales strategy sessions in which we delivered content and led the group in interactive, strategic problem solving. **Our mission was to help Google improve individual performance and business results.**

In every direction, the STEP UP philosophy was in action. Google was already wildly successful. The organization had been raising the bar on results since its inception. Yet, here Google was asking us to help the organization STEP UP.

One of my colleagues delivered the lead-off session. While he was a highly competent trainer and facilitator, Google's response was "good but not great." You see, top performing organizations do not settle for good. They demand greatness. My colleague's performance was good, but not great. He had not connected with them, and they had not connected with him. As a result, **Google was on the brink of canceling the entire $1,000,000 roll-out.**

I was on deck to deliver the second session. Talk about pressure. I fully understood the risks, rewards and requirements to succeed. I had to STEP UP and I did. It was a home run. My years of preparation were paying off in a big way. Google was delighted with my work and their organization's results. They decided to have a third session and asked me to deliver it. I hit another home run, and that cemented the relationship.

———

The difference between ordinary and
extraordinary is that little extra.
ZIG ZIGLAR

In the end, Google got the performance improvement it was looking for, so they were very happy. Not only did Google keep the program going, it was expanded internationally. So, Huthwaite was happy. Google also requested Huthwaite assign me exclusively to deliver all future sessions. **This was like stepping up to the plate and hitting back-to-back-to-back home runs in the World Series of Training Results!**

What exactly did I do that others had not? During each session, I had to continuously evaluate where I was, where I needed to be and figure out how to close the gap quickly. Where most trainers look at their audience, I looked into the audience and accurately evaluated if that person was "getting it" or "getting tired of it." Essentially, I was evaluating each business executive while at the same time delivering information, fielding questions and thinking five steps ahead. In short, I stepped up!

And then? I'll tell you more about me later, but for now, let's go to our broader discussion about unleashing your potential.

THE LAW OF ATTR*ACTION*

You attract what you do about what you think.
DANIEL GRISSOM

We've all heard of the Law of Attraction. It says, you attract what you think about. But, *do your results in sales and leadership support this definition?* Mine have not. Hey, I thought about getting straight A's during my school days and having the physique of a body builder, but neither happened. *Why is that?*

It's because The Law of Attraction is a misnomer. It's really The Law of Attr*action*, which is a combination of attraction and *action*. You don't attract what you think about, but you attract *what you do* about what you think. **The key is action!**

And when you do take action, you must give your best to attract the best. Think about it. Likely, when you aimed for an A+ in school you got that result. But, when you aimed for a B+ or less, you got an incongruent result. *Why is it that only A+ standards produce congruent results?*

Your Standards	Your Results
A+	A+
B+	C+
C+	D+

First, it's because when you don't give your best, the universe reciprocates by giving you a substandard result. **The universe rewards excellence**

and reproves average intitiative! It's just that simple. Consider the parable of the talents. Here's my paraphrasing of this biblical story. Once, there was a Master who entrusted large some of money (talents) to his three workers. The Master gave these talents according to the ability of each worker. The Master expected each worker to invest these talents and maximize their potential, while he was away.

What happened? When the Master returned he discovered that only two of the workers developed their talents. He was pleased. The 3rd worker, *who "just thought" about taking action and giving his best,* was severely rebuked. *Why?* It's because he failed to take action. He failed to develop his God-given talents. *Could you be sitting on your sales and leadership talents?*

This was unacceptable to the Master and this worker was thrown into utter darkness. And, his talents were given to the other workers that had taken action. *Do you get it?* Although, the 3rd worker *thought* about taking action, he attracted rebuke because of his lack of actions, not because of his well-meaning thoughts.

Second, **it's because the universe is inviting you to step out of your comfort zone.** *What's a comfort zone?* It's a place that you go to relax and sometimes fall asleep. The universe presents you with a substandard result because it wants you to wake up. It beckons you to expand your comfort zone and step up. The universe knows that the comfort zone is really the danger zone because it's suppressing your God-given potential.

Third, **it's because the formula for "achieving excellence" is clearer than that for "achieving average".** In other words, the requirements for transformation (your best effort) are clearer than those for modification (your second best effort). Think about that for a minute. *Have you ever tried to lose two pounds, but then struggled to decide what you could eat or do to achieve this goal?* But in comparison, when you decided to STEP UP and lost 10 pounds, the do's and don'ts were crystal clear. You see, transformation is an A+ standard, which produces excellent results. But, modification is the equivalent of a B+ standard, which produces average results.

In summary, the law of attr*action* commands you to raise your standards, take action and unleash your potential in sales and life. The universe demands you step out of your comfort zone. It invites you to STEP UP!

SALES MASTERY

Often, we don't need more skill. We need more will!
DANIEL GRISSOM

Every year, Fortune 500 companies spend millions of dollars on sales training with a commitment to improving performance and results. The supposition underlying most of these investments is that mediocre sales performance is primarily due to lack of effective sales skills and/or strategies. Sadly, these factors are rarely the root cause of sales ineffectiveness. The reality is that sales success is an inside job.

Consider the sales mastery model. The foundation is the "Self" tier, which includes your mental toughness, self-discipline and commitment to excellence. The "Strategies" tier refers to your organizational strategies to execute with excellence and clearly articulate your company's value proposition. And the "Skills" portion refers to your ability to connect, communicate and compel the client into action during a series of sales calls.

Sales Mastery

Which level is the most important for improving your sales results?

Well, all three levels are important, but studies have shown that the "Self" level is the most critical. *Why?* Simple. It's because **your sales results can only grow to the extent that you do!** Think about it. You need more self-actualization and less self-limitation. You should aspire for more self-mastery, so that you can achieve more sales mastery.

The reality is that sales mastery is predicated upon self mastery. And, in all of us, there is a God-given potential to be masterful. *Have you unleashed that potential?* As the chart below illustrates, stepping up to the next level positions you to achieve superior results and ensures competitive advantage.

Self Mastery	Sales Results
Excellent	Excellent
Good	Average
Average	Poor

Is it time for you to STEP UP to the next level?

SELF MASTERY

By mastering this one thing, you gain access to all other things!
OLD PROVERB

How do you achieve self mastery? There are three actions that you can take to eliminate mediocrity and achieve mastery. Here they are:

First, you must STEP UP! You must apply the model to all areas of sales and leadership. *Why?* It's because these are the six steps that make 80% of the difference in the achievement of results. You see, the difference between mediocrity and mastery is not hundred new actions. It's a half dozen actions in a few key areas. Think about it. *What's the difference between an A+ student and B+ student? What's the difference between the winning and losing team in the playoffs? What's the difference between you closing the sale versus your competition?* Usually, it's just a few focused actions.

Second, **you must pursue mastery.** *Why is that?* It's because **mastering anything requires you to take command of the main thing – yourself.** Consider this. *Why do companies spend thousands of dollars trying to capture the graduates with the highest grade point averages?* It's because they know that in order to master the material and achieve a superior GPA, that person had to first master themselves. They had to discipline themselves. They had to set higher standards. They had to STEP UP! The recruiting organization covets these graduates, not for their school mastery, but for their self mastery. **They understand that self mastery precedes results mastery.** *What good habits have you mastered or what bad habits have mastered you?*

Last, **you must spend major time on major matters.** You cannot spend major time on the minor matters. *Have you been getting the ratios mixed up?* You must get the path to mastery and stay on it. This path requires dedication and discipline. *What's dedication?* It's total commitment. *What's discipline?* It's total commitment in action. **You see, mastery is not about perfection. It's about the application of the daily disciplines.**

What would it mean to you, your relationships and results, if you could develop more self mastery?

THE PSYCHOLOGY OF WINNING

Physical strength will make the opponent weaken and mental toughness will make him crack.
VINCE LOMBARDI
NFL Hall of Fame Coach

Top performers visualize their desired outcomes! Their success is never a surprise to them because they experienced it first in their mind. They see their success before they ever start a project. If you don't see it, I promise you no one else will either.

Put it this way, you'll never achieve a result you haven't already pre-determined in your mind. If you are thinking, "this will never work," it won't. You must see success. Envision yourself succeeding today, in your next meeting, and over the next year.

Will it always happen?

No, but you'll be stepping up for something more, and you'll find yourself succeeding more than ever before. After all, if you don't have a vision for yourself than you will fall victim to the vision that someone else has for you.

Top performers have the psychology for results. When conditions are against them, they succeed. Their psychology is geared solely for success. When two similarly talented individuals compete, psychology wins. Mental attitude will propel one of them to success. *The question is: do you have this successful psychology?*

Top performers believe they'll come out on top. Nothing is going to stop them. Their psychology is always focused on nothing less than the best. *The market is bad?* I increase my sales. *My boss sabotages my efforts?* I succeed. *The competition is too strong?* Never. I win. *Why?* Quite simply, because it all starts with me and a successful psychology.

Take a look at the following graphic. It illustrates that superior results begin with a superior psychology or belief system. A superior belief system leads to superior action and results.

Unleash Your Potential

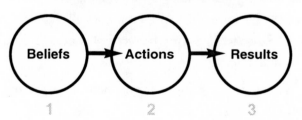

Beliefs → Actions → Results

1   2   3

Think about it.

Can a salesperson earn $250,000 with a $75,000 belief system?

Of course not! A seller can never outperform or out earn the beliefs that are inside his head. A belief is a feeling of internal certainty about the possibility of achieving a result. **The bottom line is self-limiting beliefs produce limited results while unlimited beliefs produce unlimited results.**

Let me share a true story with you about an athlete, which is a parallel for the corporate athlete, who had an unlimited belief system and achieved unbelievable results.

UNLIMITED BELIEFS

Success is 80% mindset and 20% mechanics.
TONY ROBBINS

Do you remember the story of Roger Bannister, the first person to break the four-minute mile back in 1954?

If you'll recall, the belief system at that time in track and field was that it was humanly impossible to run a mile in less than four minutes. No one had ever done it and the belief was that no one could ever do it. In fact, medical journals and documented science said that the human heart would literally explode inside the chest cavity if exerted to that rate.

But in 1954, amazingly, Roger Bannister defied the odds and broke through these limiting beliefs and ran a four-minute mile. He is a prime example of a STEP UP individual who embodies all six of the components. Think about it. **Bannister had won the race in his mind before the race had even started** in that:

1. He had an unwavering commitment to breaking the record (High Standards).

2. He had the DNA or talent to do it and he knew how to leverage his talent.

3. He was an expert evaluator – he figured out where the gap was and how to close it.

4. He prepared, practiced, and broke the record several times in his mind (he visualized the end result).

5. He took action – he ran the race and broke the record.

6. He hired a coach to help him unleash his potential.

After Bannister broke the record in 1954, guess what happened just one short year later?

Thirty-seven other runners broke it. And the year after that over 200 people broke it. And today we see youths in high school and college breaking it all the time.

So what really changed back in 1954?

It was his self-belief about what was possible that led to the breakthrough results. Bannister had the hunger and a remarkable psychology that helped him achieve a remarkable result. It was his mindset, not his mechanics, that was the difference.

What's your four-minute mile for you this year?

What's the one belief that if you shifted could unleash your potential and explode your sales results?

PLAY TO WIN!

You can't climb uphill by thinking downhill thoughts.
SOURCE UNKNOWN

The other night I was watching ESPN and a program called "The

Battle Lines." It focused on the Master's Tournament of 1986 – one of the most coveted sporting events in the world.

A spry and young European named Seve Ballesteros was leading the field by a landslide. On his heels were prime-time golfers Tom Kite and Greg Norman, and bringing up the rear was an over-the-hill 46-year-old golfer named Jack Nicklaus.

According to the story, Nicklaus was so many strokes behind the rest of the field that CBS network asked its cameramen to adjust their attention to the other golfers because "Nicklaus' game was irrelevant."

Then what happened?

The momentum shifted! Old man Nicklaus made a couple of unexpected birdies on the "back nine" and the crowd began to take note. Simultaneously, the other golfers that were leading the field began to play it safe. In doing so, they began to lose their mental edge and committed errors that lost strokes. They began **"playing not to lose" versus continuing to "play to win!"**

And then?

Nicklaus hit a few unbelievable shots and the crowd erupted. The gallery's cheers enveloped the other golfers and began to affect their focus and psychology. As one of them later said, "I began to wait for things to happen, instead of making things happen." These frontrunners had become fearful. **This was their fatal flaw.**

In the end, Jack Nicklaus won the 1986 Masters! He did so by unleashing his potential, playing with no fear and playing to win.

Playing it safe is Risky.

What's the message?

The message is in **that in order to unleash your potential you've got to win the inner game first and play to win instead of playing not to lose.**

DIVIDE OR MULTIPLY?

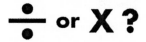

Is the unleashing of potential your responsibility or the responsibility of your employer?

Of course, **the primary responsibility for unleashing your potential and taking action is yours!** Top performers know this and act on this reality about results.

You'll find them constantly stepping up to take the classes, reading the books and proactively preparing themselves for superior results. Average performers do some of this, but too often they wait for their organization to provide training and development. They may get the book their company recommended, but they probably decide not to read it. They learn about the seminars that can take their results to the next level, but decide they'll enroll only if their company is willing to pay for it.

What impact does self-reliance have on results?

Well, let me put it this way. If you take responsibility for your own self-development, **you can multiply your potential results by two because self-initiative has a multiplier effect on results.** In contrast, if you depend on your organization to develop you, then you must divide your potential results by two because relying on others will have a reductive effect on your results. *Get it?* Your performance and potential will be maximized when you step up and take responsibility for your own refinement and results.

What's the difference between top performers and average performers?

Top performers are committed to their own success and invest in their #1 product or themselves because they know that business growth cannot exceed personal growth. So if you want more of the former you must invest in the latter.

How committed are you to your own success?

EXCELLENCE IN EXECUTION

*Execution is the great unaddressed issue in the business world
today. Its absence is the single biggest obstacle to success and
the cause of most of the disappointments that are
mistakenly attributed to other causes.*
LARRY BOSSIDY
Execution

Booz Allen surveyed over 50,000 global organizations and asked them specifically whether they had the ability to quickly translate important strategic and operational decisions into action. More than half (54%) said they did not have the ability to quickly unleash their organizational potential.[19]

Here are some of the complaints captured in the study:

- Everyone agrees on a course of action, but nothing changes.

- There goes another opportunity while we wait for a decision.

- It's a great idea, but it will never happen.

- The businesses and functions just aren't working together to get results.

- I don't feel motivated to go the extra mile.

- What's in it for me?

- We have the right strategy and a clear implementation plan; we just can't seem to execute.

Do any of these sound familiar to you? Do they conjure images of under-achieving team members? Those statements represent counterproductive behaviors that undermine any organization's success.

Think about it. **The ability to unleash and execute is not something you can hire or mandate. It is inherent, embedded in the organization's**

---

19. Booz Allen, *Organizational DNA, The Resilience Report*

genes and DNA. And of course, organizational DNA is the aggregate of the DNA of the individuals in the organization. So, to ensure you have an organization that can execute and break through to the next level, you must ensure you have sellers and leaders who can execute as we discussed extensively in Chapter 2.

THE KNOWING-DOING GAP

I have never heard anything about the resolutions of the Apostles,
but a great deal about their Acts
H. MANN

It's one thing to know what to do, quite another to actually do it. This *Knowing-Doing Gap* exists in organizations and it exists in individuals.

We have vast resources of knowledge available to us, but we're often plagued with an inertia that manifests by confusing knowing with doing. The result is we know too much and do too little.

We confuse talking and planning with action. We think that making a decision is the same as action. We think that measuring things is action.

Although talking, planning, measuring and decision-making are all important elements of success, **it is essential we not confuse activity with achievement.**

Jeffrey Pheffer and Robert Sutton, authors of *The Knowing-Doing Gap*, offer these two sadly true and sadly typical examples of organizations with knowing-doing gaps.

1. An international metals and oil company was posting terrible numbers – sales and profits were down, as was share price. The company's senior executives were mortified by the results; they knew major changes in strategy and operations were imperative.

Their response: to spend at least half their time in darkened rooms, watching elaborate presentations about the company's performance.

2. Faced with a worrisomely slow time-to-market for its new products, a large furniture company conducted a careful benchmarking study. The results were clear: a project-based organizational structure would help solve the problem. But more than a year later, the company had not instituted a single change. Senior executives, although uniformly supportive of the idea of restructuring the organization, were still discussing it in meetings that ended with decisions – decisions to have more meetings.

What causes the knowing-doing gap? Authors Pheffer and Sutton say the cause is often traced to a basic human propensity – the willingness to let talk substitute for action.[19]

What then makes people willing to substitute talk for action?

Three things:

1. **I believe the number one reason is Fear** – Fear of taking initiative, making a mistake, and either not being perfect, or getting reprimanded for taking the wrong action. Think about it. Talk, unlike action, isn't very risky. The person who makes no decisions can hardly be blamed for having made a bad one.

2. **The second reason people don't take action is a lack of structure for action.** In fact, some organizations install a structure for nonaction by punishing employees who take action. If an organization follows up on plans so they get implemented, if they train for and reward action, then chances are they'll see more action.

3. **The third reason people don't take action is that they're not mentally wired for action.** Imagine a continuum with Proactive on one side and Passive on the other. For every situation in life, each of us falls somewhere along that continuum. If I am passive in sales situations, for example, I will tend to think more than act. I'll prefer to learn disproportionately more than I take action on.

You must turn your knowing into doing.

How to close the knowing-doing gap?

Simple. Stop talking, stop pondering, stop researching and take action. **Quit talking about what you're going to do, and just do it!**

YOU COULD. YOU SHOULD. BUT DON'T?

You could do it. You should do it, but you don't do it.
That's a formula for disaster.
JIM ROHN

You could take action. You should take action. But you don't take action. *Why is that?*

One of the things individuals and organizations do which severely hampers our results is to delay doing something. **Procrastination is the "death rattle" to results.** We delay taking action, or we never quite finish what we start. We get distracted and caught up in other things. We might even make excuses for why we can't or don't take action or complete what we start.

There are two types of procrastination.

The first type of procrastination is behavioral. This is characterized by distraction and avoidance. According to Joseph Ferrari, author of *Procrastination and Task Avoidance*, procrastinators often delay projects so they'll have an excuse if they don't do well. Ferrari says, "Procrastinators view their self-worth as based solely on ability at a task. So their logic says, "If I never finish the task, you can never judge my ability."

Delaying projects also offers procrastinators a handy excuse if they don't do well. "They'd rather create the impression that they lacked effort than ability," says Ferrari. "They can blame it on the lack of time."[20]

In fact, they will often handicap themselves to guarantee an excuse if they perform poorly.

The second type of procrastination is decisional. This is the pattern of postponing a decision when dealing with conflicts and choices. People with high decisional procrastination are considered perfectionists. That's a smoke screen. They often seek perfection because it gives them an excuse to take longer to make decisions.

A fascinating explanation of procrastination comes from Clarry Lay, PhD, a professor of psychology at York University in Toronto and creator of the General Procrastination Scale. Lay believes that procrastinators simply have a different level of conscientiousness than most people. Put simply: They think and act in terms of "wishes and dreams" while non-procrastinators focus on "oughts and obligations," he says. They are also neurotically disorganized in their thinking, he says, making them forgetful and less likely to plan well.[20]

Regardless of the cause, the results are the same – weak! You simply can't procrastinate and expect superior results.

Furthermore, a person who procrastinates eventually is overcome by stress and guilt. The longer you put off doing something, the bigger that thing becomes in your mind. And it doesn't go away; it keeps coming back. As soon as the first deadline is missed, the project or goal no longer has integrity. It's a lesser goal with diminished expectations. On the other hand, since mastery is the steady improvement over time, your performance and results can only get better by making the best decision possible for right now. Procrastination says, "I'll do tomorrow." Mastery says, "I'll do it right now to the best of my ability."

You have two choices:

---

20. *The Danger in Delay*, David Jacobson, WebMD, November 27, 2000

1. Procrastination and Excuses, which lead to Mediocrity
2. Discipline and Execution, which lead to Mastery

YOU COULD. YOU SHOULD. AND YOU DID!

———•———

You've got to bring it to get it!
MAMA

What can you do to move from Procrastination to Implementation?

1. **Break up the chunks.**

   Oftentimes procrastination results from trying to work with too big a chunk. Your goal is too big, maybe even overwhelming. If you want to lose 50 pounds for example, start by focusing on losing 10 pounds. Once you've achieved that goal, then set your sights on the next 10 pounds. If you're aiming to work on the treadmill for an hour each day, start by doing it for 10 minutes. Action is simply part of a process.

2. **Take action now.**

   Imperfect action today is better than perfect tomorrow. Once you take the first step, you'll find the second and third step will come more easily. You'll begin developing a pattern, a habit, a discipline that will help you achieve successively larger goals.

3. **Leverage the power of NOW.**

   Now. Own. Won! The message of these interchangeable words is take action now, take ownership for results now and you can expect to win more and lose less.

———•———

Champions do daily what amateurs do occasionally.

THE TOP VS. AVERAGE PERFORMERS

Average is being at the Top of the bottom!
MAMA

What separates Top Performers from those who struggle?

Top Performers are doers. They opt for action now versus perfection later. Top Performers have a results discipline while Average Performers have excuses and tend to procrastinate.

Top Performers have a sense of urgency, while Average Performers tend to get complacent and comfortable.

Top Performers have a strong belief in their ability to achieve results. They recognize the importance of the 80% mental component and put their focus there. Average Performers focus on the 20% skill component, often underestimating the importance of the mental game.

Here's a summary:

Top Performers	Average Performers
Know and Do	The Knowing-Doing Gap
Work Smarter	Work Harder
Price of Discipline	Cost of Regret
The Beliefs	The Skills
I Must Do	I Should Do

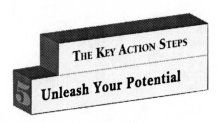

Here are the key action steps of this chapter:

1. **Take Responsibility for Unleashing Your Potential.**

   If you take responsibility, you'll achieve superior results. If you defer the responsibility to others, your results will suffer.

2. **Know and Do.**

   Be aware of Knowing-Doing gaps and close them. Recognize procrastination tendencies and change your behavior to ensure you take action and complete tasks.

3. **Create a List of Your Shoulds and Musts.**

   A "should" says I'll do it when it's convenient. A "must" says I'll do it because I'm committed. Transform your top three shoulds into musts.

4. **Increase Your Diligence and Discipline.**

   Take consistent action daily. Hold yourself accountable. You must pay the price of discipline or the cost of regret.

5. **Strengthen Your Mental Toughness.**

   Listen to the conversation going on in your head. *Is it serving you or sabotaging you?* Consider modeling the beliefs and behaviors of those that are achieving the results you desire.

Step Six

INVEST IN COACHING

He was a coach that demanded excellence. He expected you to come out and play 100% every night. He'd prepare offensively and defensively. Coach Riley would put you in a position to win every night.
MAGIC JOHNSON
NBA Hall of Famer

Have you forgotten a Step on the Road to Superior Results?

Coaching helps you win more and lose less. Coaching helps you make those small distinctions and adjustments in your strategy that can make the big difference in results. Too often, coaching is the forgotten and missed step on the road to results. I purposefully "forgot" to put the coaching "C" into the "STEP UP" acronym to symbolically make the point.

If you take a look at the world's top performers across all professions, you'll find a common denominator – the best use coaches. Think about it. Ali had Angelo, Jordan had Jackson and Robbins had Rohn!

The world's great performers are continuously trying to improve their skills; that's how they reach such a high level of performance. And the means to their skill level is inevitably great coaching.

The reason we need coaches is that we simply can't see ourselves. Very few humans possess what's known in acting as a "transcendental ego," the ability to clearly see yourself in real time as though you're looking through someone else's eyes. In other words, many top performers do not have a clue what it is they do that makes them so successful.

We need another person to scrutinize our strengths with a critical eye and help us build on them. We need the assistance of a world-class communicator who can recognize our weaknesses and can inform us about them in a way that encourages us, rather than deflates us. We need a mind's eye outside ourselves to help us understand ourselves today and who we can be tomorrow – then make sure we get there. **Coaches can help you make the small distinctions that can save you years of time, effort and frustration.**

COACHING

- Helps ensure you maintain a results discipline.
- Ensures you keep your commitment to yourself.
- Empowers you to get the results you want on a consistent basis.

PERSONAL COACHING

Great coaching helps you to keep the promises you've made with yourself.
TONY ROBBINS

Here's an analogy that mirrors the lives of many corporate athletes, like you and me. It's a story about a world-class athlete that had the raw talent, but initially failed to unleash his potential because of one missing step. *Can you guess what that is?*

It was 1995 and our athlete was considered to be one of the top runners in the world. He had world-class speed and commitment. His eyes were on the prize of making the Olympic team, then winning the Gold Medal in 1996 in Atlanta.

In preparation for the Olympics trails, he committed to give his best and coach himself. *Sound familiar?* Initially, he was self-disciplined and self-motivated. He pushed himself to get stronger and run faster. But in time, his self-discipline dipped just a little, but it was no big deal. *How could small dip make a big difference?*

Fast forward, the long-awaited day for the Olympic trails had arrived. On your mark, get set, go! Our man was off to the races. *Who won? Who made the team?* Amazingly, our runner lost the race and got cut from the team! He had fallen short of achieving his dreams. *But, how could that be? The others had less potential?*

Fast forward again, this time to the Olympic Games in 1996. *Where's our runner?* He's sitting in the stands. He's watching others win his gold medal and recognition! *Sound familiar?* As he sat in the stand as a spectator he asked himself, *"What did these runners have that I didn't?"* The answer to his question was Coaching!

Unbeknownst to him, his competitors had hired personal coaches to hold them accountable to their daily goals and help them step up to the next level. *Do you get it?* **The other runners had less potential, but they won because of better coaching.** *Is your team being outplayed or just outcoached?*

Our runner promised himself that he'd never fall short of his goals again. He'd hire someone to give him feedback. He'd hire someone to encourage, challenge and remind him to live up to his full potential. And, professional coaching would be the means to that end! As a corporate athlete, *who is helping you live up to your full potential?*

Feedback is the breakfast of champions.
MAMA

Now, let's fast forward to the year 2000 when the Olympics were held in Australia. The challenges and competitors were similar, but his results were different. Our man made the team, won the 60 yard dash and became the fastest man in the world! *If you had a coach for the next 12 months that held you personally accountable, then what new results could you achieve?*

Do you know this runner's name? His name was Maurice Green. The perfect parallel to sellers and leaders, like you and me. **The benefit of coaching is that it raises your standards and ensures that you keep the promises you made with yourself.** It can give you the structure and strategy to unleash your potential. **You know that there is a part of you that has the potential for greatness.** *Have you unleashed it?*

Sadly, too many corporate athletes and entrepreneurial tri-athletes try to go it alone, and it shows in their results. I know first-hand how coaching can impact your performance and results because I've had sales coaches, book coaches and speaking coaches. *Do you have a results coach? Should you?* If you would like coaching, then drop me an email at **daniel@phdin-results.com** and I'll give you a complimentary coaching session.

By the way, parents are coaches too. Think about it. Didn't your Mom, Dad and/or Grandparents help you raise your standards, make effective decisions and step up to the next level? I know mine did, especially, mama. She was my first coach and helped me "live up to my potential" and "keep the promises I made with myself." That was the magic of mama!

Behind every great Champion there is a great Coach!

THINK. ACT. WIN!

The ultimate aim of coaching is to help you to think differently, act consistently and win convincingly!
DANIEL GRISSOM

As we read in the previous example, coaches and leaders have a multiplier effect on performance and results. Investing in a coach can take several forms. You can hire a professional or get coaching by reading a book, attending a seminar or being a part of a mastermind group. You see, coaching is just about having a thought partner that can help you think, act and win! *How does coaching affect the results model?*

As the visual illustrates, effective coaching is often the catalyst to helping individuals and organizations reach their maximum potential. At the self level, effective coaching can help you develop the mental edge required to achieve superior results in sales and life. At the strategies level, coaching can help you develop the action plans to win more and lose less. And finally, at the skills level, effective coaching can help you develop the mechanics to execute with excellence. In summary, effective coaching can help you think, act and win!

THE BUSINESS CASE FOR COACHING

*The goal of coaching is the goal of good management –
to make the most of an organization's valuable resources.*
THE HARVARD BUSINESS REVIEW

Coaching is a process of equipping people with the tools, knowl-edge, and opportunities they need in order to develop themselves and become more successful. A company's potential for results depends on receiving the benefit of every employee's ability to produce those results.

Let's examine three case studies that further make the business case for coaching:

1. Xerox Corporation's Newcastle branch had been a poor perform-ing unit for several years. Conventional classroom training had not improved results, so Xerox management decided to implement a two-month, on-the-job coaching program. The results – greatly improved productivity. The branch, which had been trailing at 16th out of 17 in productivity ratings, moved to top place. Even more significant, from needing 48 calls on customers to achieve an order, the branch moved to taking an order from every 24 calls.[21]

2. Michigan-based Triad Performance Technologies, Inc. studied and evaluated the effects of a coaching intervention on a group of regional and district sales managers within a large telecom organ-ization. This third party research study cited a 10:1 return on investment, in less than one year, for this organization that invest-ed in coaching. The study found that the following business out-comes were directly attributable to the coaching intervention:

   • Top performing staff, who were considering leaving the organization, were retained, resulting in reduced turnover, increased revenue, and improved customer satisfaction.

---

21. Neil Rackham, *The Coaching Controversy, Corporate Investment in Training Sees Greater Pay-offs with the Integration of Coaching,* Huthwaite.com

- A positive work environment was created, focusing on strategic account development and higher sales volume.

- Customer revenues and customer satisfaction were improved due to fully staffed and fully functioning territories.

- Revenues were increased due to managers improving their performance and exceeding their goals.

3. In a study by MetrixGlobal, the coaching of corporate executives in a multi-national telecommunications company produced a 529% return on investment and significant intangible benefits to the business. Including the financial benefits from employee retention, coaching boosted the overall R.O.I. to 788%.[22]

INVEST NOW OR PAY LATER?

*Without coaching, very few people can maintain
a newly acquired skill.*
NEIL RACKHAM
The Coaching Controversy

Perhaps the strongest argument for coaching is this – However good your skills training in the classroom, unless it is followed up on the job, will lose its effectiveness.

According to a study by the Xerox Corporation, **87 percent of the desired skills change was lost without follow-up coaching.** The implication is that, no matter how good the classroom training is, the effectiveness is lost without on-the-job reinforcement.[21] In other words, **if you pay for training and forego the follow-up then you're suboptimizing the results of your training dollars.**

---

22. *he Business Case for Consulting,* LeadershipAdvantage.com

Results Coaching

Training and Coaching

Training Only

No Training or Coaching

RESULTS

TIME

Look at the graphic which crystallizes the effects of coaching. If you have no training or coaching, results are minimal, period. With training, you get better results initially, but they drop off. When you combine training and coaching, you achieve maximum results.

Will you invest in coaching now or will you pay later?

THE FORTUNE IS IN THE FOLLOW-UP

A client recently said, "the fortune is in the follow-up." I love that because it's so true. In order to achieve sustainable results and see the impact on your bottom line, you have to follow up. **You have to help individuals integrate new skills until they become new habits.** That is how performance improvement works.

Learning and integrating new skills can be difficult and frustrating. I know firsthand, having labored to improve my own performance. Improvements typically are not immediate and often decline while the new skills are being practiced. This lack of improvement causes many people to give up on the new skills and revert to their old ways. It is this exact point where the **coaching can resuscitate results.**

Actually, when performance dips, what's happening is that the new skills are working their way from conscious competence to unconscious competence. **Coaching is the only way to make sure that the skills make the journey.**

Have you ever made a New Year's resolution?

Here's what often happens. You get motivated, step up and take action. You see some improvement in the short term, but after a few weeks your commitment and results dip.

I call that the "Discipline Dip." The Discipline Dip is similar to the process of lifting weights to strengthen a weak muscle. Most people give up and start working on muscles that are already strong. When you lose focus and forget to work on the goal, your mind is reverting to the stronger neuro pathway. The result: you regress back into your old patterns and behavior.

Again, this is the exact point where coaching can raise the bar on results. **Coaching helps you get through the lag time – the time between early commitment and results.** Think about it. You've developed patterns of behavior over many years and it's unrealistic to think you'll change them overnight – no matter how much motivation you can stir up. **It's essential to maintain the momentum during the "discipline dip."** And when you don't have a coach, your chances of success are greatly limited. That is why so many New Year's resolutions and post seminar promises go unfulfilled. **The solution is to maintain momentum via Coaching because it enables you to transform new skills into new habits.**

THE LEADERSHIP CHALLENGE

Does this sound familiar?

> Your sales team needs you.
>
> Your key competitors are after you.
>
> And Wall Street is watching you.
>
> The market's message is clear: "Step Up or Get Stepped On!"
>
> This is the Leadership Challenge.

The corporate coach's critical condition is exacerbated by the fact that many of the organizations do not have a coaching culture. This is evidenced when organizations investing major time measuring what I call the "lagging indicators" of results, like revenue reports, but investing minor time improving what I call the "leading indicators" of results, like talent development.

Regretfully, most organizations focus more on developing revenue and less focus on developing the revenue producer – their talent. This is suboptimal because business growth is always commensurate with personal growth. In short, **in order for there to be more business development organizations must invest more in talent development.** And coaching is the means to that end.

EXCELLENCE IN LEADERSHIP

The quality of leadership, more than any other single factor, determines the success or failure of a team.
FRED FIELDER
The Leadership Match Concept

Steven J. Stowell and Matt M. Starcevich in *The Coach – Creating Partnerships for a Competitive Advantage* explain the changing role of leadership:

The new job of the leader is to coach, develop, train, delegate, facilitate and run interference – rather than doing all the planning, organizing and directing from an authoritative base.[23]

That said, the authors also note:

Coaching is the most uncomfortable, avoided, and mishandled of all management tasks.

Here's how Larry Bossidy describes coaching in *Execution!*:

How good would a sports team be if the coach spent all of his time in his office making deals for new players, while delegating actual coaching to an assistant? A coach is effective because he's constantly observing players individually and collectively on the field and in the locker

---

23. *The Coach: Creating Partnerships for a Competitive Edge* by Steven Stowell, Matt M. Stracevich

room. That's how he gets to know his players and their capabilities, and how they get firsthand the benefit of his experience, wisdom and expert feedback. It's no different for a business leader.

The effective coach often does not have to tell people what to do; she asks questions as a way to help them figure out what to do on their own. In this way she coaches them, passing on her experience as a leader and educating them to think in new ways.

------·------

You cannot change people, but you can empower
people to change themselves.

THE 1% DIFFERENCE

------·------

You can't win this year's championship with last year's strategy!
PAT RILEY

Great leaders are the embodiment of the STEP UP model in that they are able to help teams improve results. They do so by raising standards of the team, selecting the right players, evaluating performance gaps, preparing for future challenges and unleashing the full potential of each person.

Consider Pat Riley, former Coach of the L.A. Lakers and current Coach of the Miami Heat. Riley is one of the great coaches in NBA history and has coached some of the greatest players of all time. Riley is able to motivate his players to commit to excellence and step up to the next level.

Think back to the 1986 season when Riley had a major challenge on his hands. Many of the Lakers' players had given what they thought was their best season in the previous year, but still had lost to the Boston Celtics.

In search of a **strategy** to get his players to step up and achieve their potential, he challenged them to make small improvements. He invited all the players to improve by at least 1% over their previous personal best in five areas of their performance. *How could a small improvement make a major difference in results?* Well, think about 12 players improving their performance by 1% in five key areas. The combined effort created a team that was 60% more effective than before! And a 10% improvement in team performance would likely be enough to win another championship.

Riley convinced the members of his team to raise the bar and unleash their full potential. *The results?* Most of them increased by at least 5% and many of them by as much as 50%. According to Pat Riley, 1987 turned out to be their easiest season ever.

You see, the leadership difference is your ability to influence teams and individuals to make the small changes in behavior that make a big difference in results. Often, great coaching and leadership is the difference between winning and losing. As a leader, *are you making a difference?*

THE LEADERSHIP SOLUTION

Leadership is the art of acomplishing more than the science of management says is possible.
THE LEADERSHIP SECRETS OF COLIN POWELL

What's the solution?

You are! Think about it. **The effectiveness of salespeople rarely rises above the effectiveness of the coach.** That means that you, the leader, must

STEP UP your performance. You must be willing to raise your standards, ensure your DNA is aligned with the job, ask quality questions, make effective evaluations, prepare to win and unleash your full potential. In order to lead others effectively you must first consistently lead yourself.

THE WINNER WITHIN

Self-leadership comes first, because effective leadership starts on the inside. Before you can hope to lead anyone else, you have to know yourself and what you need to be successful. Self knowledge gives you perspective.
KEN BLANCHARD
Leading At A Higher Level

Effective leadership of others starts with looking at yourself – who you are, what you stand for and how to take initiative when you don't have a position of power. In other words, you must consistently lead yourself before you can effectively develop others. The key is self-leadership. Then, you should identify the strategies and skills for building high performance teams.

An effective results strategy is to customize your coaching to the unique needs of your teams as you'll find out in the next section.

CHAMPIONSHIP COACHING

People are unique and must be managed, coached and supported
in a way that capitalizes on their uniqueness.
TARGET TRAINING INTERNATIONAL

In order to maximize the performance of each corporate athlete, the leader must understand the specific strengths and challenges of each person on his team. The leader should know the do's and don'ts for effectively managing, motivating and communicating with each individual. You must accurately understand your people before you can effectively coach. *Why?* **Because you can't coach what you don't understand!**

You must accurately understand your people before
you can effectively coach them.

Here's one of my favorite examples about a coach that had to accurately understand his player before he could effectively coach the player:

Mack Brown, Head Coach of the University of Texas football team, learned this lesson when he stopped trying to "fix" quarterback Vince Young.

Coach Brown had tried to fix Young's three-quarter throwing skills and was unsuccessful. Coach Brown had tried to turn Young into a traditional "drop back and pass" quarterback. Coach Brown was frustrated because Young's performance was initially declining. Amazingly, it was when Coach Brown began to better understand Young's standards, DNA and ability to effectively evaluate he quit trying to fix Young. And in doing so, his quarterback became a stellar performer and the Longhorns became the #1 football team in the country, winning the 2006 National Championship Game against the previously undefeated USC Trojans.

How effective are you at identifying the specific needs of your sellers and getting the most from them?

CULTURE OF COACHING

Profit is the applause you get for taking care of your clients and creating a motivating environment for your people.
KEN BLANCHARD
Leading at a Higher Level

Performance improvement is not an event, it's a process which requires a coaching culture to ensure your people are constantly learning and growing.

What are the key characteristics of coaching culture?

1. The culture is learning-focused and performance-driven, and there is explicit acknowledgment that coaching is a key component.

2. In a learning culture, employees are exposed to coaching on a regular, or even daily basis.

3. Desired behaviors are "modeled" or displayed by leaders and managers.

4. Coaching is embedded in the reward system.

Here's how the Center for Creative Leadership defines a Coaching Culture:

A coaching culture is an organizational setting in which not only formal coaching occurs, but also most or a large segment of individuals in the organization practice coaching behaviors as a means of relating to, supporting and influencing each other. Formal coaching engagements or relationships, whether with professional internal or external coaches, are only a part of a larger quilt-work of relating through coaching behaviors.[24]

Organizational support of coaching initiatives consists of a wide range of responsibilities, including: removing roadblocks that impede the process; implementing a system that facilitates the process; and ensuring that learning is aligned with organizational priorities.

What does that last thought mean? In addition to their responsibility to create the learning culture, leaders also have a responsibility to advocate, promote, reinforce and reward coaching and learning behaviors.

Here are more benefits of coaching and its culture:

Coaching culture sustains results

Coaching is the key to helping individuals and organizations sustain performance and results.

Coaching enables you to do more with less

A coaching culture is a cost-effective way to improve performance while enabling the organization to do more with less – smaller staff, smaller budgets and shorter deadlines.

In most organizations it would be cost-prohibitive for everybody in the organization to have a formal coach. Creating a social norm, where everyone acts like a coach some of the time, achieves the same end at a fraction of the cost.

Learning by helping others

In order to execute coaching behaviors, people must develop and practice a mental frame of reference where they are committed to allowing coaching to enter their lives. They must also be committed to focusing on improvement as a way to benefit the organization as a whole.

That last thought benefits both individuals and the organization in two ways. First, as people interact with each other from this perspective, they

---

24. The Center for Creative Leadership, *The Changing Nature of Leadership*

motivate each other to improve their behavior. Second, practicing this point of view facilitates people in motivating themselves to improve their own behavior.

Increased job satisfaction

In my experience, **people who contribute to coaching become self-motivated.** They become more satisfied with their jobs, and their morale improves. When your organization is populated by those people, your structure becomes one of strength, based on cooperative and collaborative professional relationships.

A license to learn

In order to execute coaching behaviors, **people must develop and practice** a mental frame of reference where they are committed to allowing coaching to enter their lives. They must also be committed to focusing on improvement as a way to benefit the organization as a whole.

That last thought benefits bth individuals and the organization in two ways. First, as people interact with each other from this perspective, they motivate each other to improve their behavior. Second, practicing this point of view facilitates people in motivating themselves to improve their own behavior.

HIRE WINNERS

Like the people they mentor and coach, all leaders and managers are charged with doing more with less. In situations when you can't coach everyone, **the best thing you can do is hire people who are able to self-coach.** Coaching really begins with the effective selection of salespeople that are self-motivated to be successful.

It works this way. If you hire talent with high standards and the right DNA, then they will coach themselves, and implement their improved skills and know-how.

What is self-driven coaching?

It's when a salesperson proactively seeks coaching through various sources: other people, books, seminars, tip teams, teleconferences, web casts and videos. People who can coach themselves don't wait for the organization to assign them a coach and a program to follow. They go out and get it on their own. They are always looking for skills, tools, knowledge and strategies that will help them grow personally and professionally.

Can you help yourself by helping others?

Another payoff you receive is that you create a culture that is filled with people who possess the right DNA, standards and focus that will coach themselves and be able to help their peers. Then, the team is prepared to provide coaching support to each other.

The old axiom is true – **we learn best when we teach others.** This becomes a continuing, self-supporting learning spiral.

WHO TO COACH?

It takes far more energy and work to improve from incompetence to mediocrity than it takes to improve from first-rate performance to excellence. And yet, most people – especially most teachers and most organizations – concentrate on making incompetent performers into mediocre ones. Energy, resources, and time should go instead to making a competent person into a star performer.
PETER DRUCKER
Managing Oneself, Harvard Business Review

Because there is a limited amount of time and energy in every organization, it's unrealistic to think that you can, or even should, coach 100% of your people. The goal is to focus the most attention on those that can make the most difference. *So then, how do you decide which people will get the coaching?*

A typical organization breaks down something like this – 20% top performers, 20% at the bottom, and 60% somewhere in the middle. See the "Before" graphic.

Before

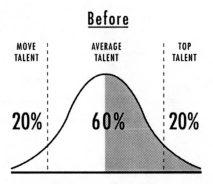

If you coach the top performers and potential top performers, then your coaching time will be maximized and your organizational performance will be optimized. You'll have more people producing the right results. See the "After" graphic.

After

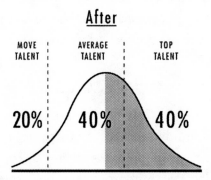

You must be discerning about who you coach to ensure you achieve the best return-on-investment of your coaching time.

WHAT TO COACH?

Ignorance is no excuse – it's the real thing.
STEVEN STOWELL
Author, *The Coach*

You should coach your talent on those factors that they perceive to be most critical to their success. So *how do you know what these critical success factors are,* you ask?

What's the most important question a coach can ask their direct reports each quarter?

I believe it's "*How can I help you be more effective?*"

Ideally, this question is asked not just in performance reviews, but as part of the ongoing dialogue between those that are leading and those being led. When asked and acted on consistently the answer to this critical question can unleash the potential of the individual and the organization.

HOW TO COACH?

There are many factors, but for the purposes of this chapter, let's limit our focus to the fundamentals. The three steps of the performance improvement process are to prepare, act and learn. **This is the same results cycle that sellers use to improve their performance and it's applicable to leadership, too.** See the following illustration.

Coaching is just like anything else. If you don't prepare or plan for it, it doesn't get done. And the review involves analyzing the coaching sessions to gather new insights for better coaching in the future.

Through coaching, you'll learn about new deals and existing deals that require your attention. **Coaching will empower you to effectively evaluate how your people are performing and enable you to make mid-course corrections to win and save deals.**

CODE OF CONDUCT

Here's a short list of leadership qualities you should be striving to attain and maintain:

- Recognize natural talents and let people be who they are (don't try to "fix" natural talents).

- Focus on effectiveness rather than efficiencies (it's about results, not activities!).

- Encourage people to take risks and learn from their mistakes.

- Support them as they make mistakes.

- Listen more than talk.

- Be candid, but provide feedback in the right size dose.

- Lead by example.

THE TOP VS. AVERAGE PERFORMERS

Average is being at the Top of the bottom!
MAMA

What separates Top Performers from those who struggle?

Here's an executive summary of Top vs. Average Performing individuals and organizations:

Top Performers	Average Performers
Customized Coaching	One Size Fits All
Partnership	Dictatorship
Invests Now	Pays Later
Mentoring Culture	Inspecting Culture
Proactive	Reactive

THE KEY ACTION STEPS

Invest in Coaching

Here are the key themes and action steps of this chapter:

1. **Invest in Coaching**

   To win deals, save deals and develop talents.

2. **Continuously Improve Yourself**

   The world's best performers are continuously improving their skills and they recognize that in order to get there and stay there they need great coaches.

3. **Focus on Feedback and Follow-up**

   87% of skills training is lost without feedback and follow-up coaching. Coaching gets you through the discipline dip while your skills are working their way from conscious competence to unconscious competence.

4. **Step Up to the New Role for Leaders**

   The new role for leaders and managers is to coach, develop, train, facilitate and run interference for the maximization of results. Coaching is the most uncomfortable, avoided and mishandled of leadership tasks.

5. **Customize Your Coaching**

   Identify the specific needs of the individuals on your team. Look below the surface and coach accordingly.

Part III

THE FINAL CONCLUSIONS

———◆———

*The greatest potential for profit to the
individual as well as the organization
resides in personal development.*
EARL NIGHTINGALE

Conclusion

ARE YOU THE CEO?

*With all the emphasis in the business press on the highest-level
executives, it is easy to overlook the need for each
employee to be his or her own CEO.*
PETER DRUCKER
The Definitive Drucker

The market's message is clear. Individual performance is the difference
between organizational profit and loss. This means that you must step up
and **become the CEO** (Chief Excellence Officer) of the privately owned
company called you. *Your mission?* It's to **win more and lose less** in business. *Your method?* It's to **achieve excellence** in all endeavors. *Your model?*
STEP UP! – the acronym for excellence.

Think about the Step Up! Model. These are the
critical success factors that directly affect your individual performance and organizational results:

- Standards
- Talents
- Evaluations
- Preparation
- Unleashing Potential
- Coaching

All of these steps are internal. They are determined by you and controlled by you. I'm not suggesting that external factors don't impact results because they do. What I am suggesting is that you have the biggest and most profound impact on your results.

For instance, think about your clients.

What is often the most important factor in a client decision in your favor?

Is it your company? Your product? Or is it you?

Of course, it's you! The client buys you first, then your product second and your company last. This has been proven thousands of times in selling/buying situations where there was a choice of vendors with similar offerings. **The deciding factor was the person, not the product or pricing or promotion.**

You are the #1 reason clients decide to buy or not. You have the biggest impact on sales results!

Want better results? **Then start by building a better you.**

JOB SECURITY

The only real security is the kind that's on the inside.
Earl Nightingale

CIRCUIT CITY cutting about 3,400 store associate jobs

CITIGROUP reportedly eyes 15,000 job cuts in reorganization plan

DELL, MOTOROLA, and IBM announce new job cuts as companies vie for market share amid falling share values, cutthroat competition and bleak economic forecasts.

Security. Some people marry for it. Banks want it before granting loans. Business professionals are looking for it. Everyone wants security, but *where can it be found?* Most business leaders would agree that **there's only one place where job security can be found and it's inside of you.** This is the only real source of security in business. And once this inner security is attained it must be maintained by improving ourselves everyday. We must improve each day if we expect to stay on top because when things stop growing they start dying. That goes for trees, plants and people.

Think about it. Everyone expects his company to grow, but *have you considered that you can grow as fast, if not faster, than your organization? Are you keeping up or ahead of your company's rate of growth?* The reality is that your company's growth is the result of its investment in business research and development each year. These investments are aimed at creating competitive advantage in the marketplace and financial security. *Should you emulate your company by investing in the personal research and development of yourself each year?*

THE VALUE OF DISCIPLINE

Excellence is not an act, it's a habit.
VINCE LOMBARDI

Consider this parable of an ancient stonecutter as a parallel to our mission to become more disciplined as sellers and leaders.

This stonecutter was responsible for cutting open giant boulders. *How did the stonecutter break open a giant boulder?* He started out with a big hammer and whacked the boulder as hard as he could.

The first time he hit it, there wasn't a scratch, not a chip – nothing! Then he pulled back the hammer and hit it again and again – 10, 20, 30 times without even a scratch.

After all this effort, the boulder did not show even the slightest crack. But the stonecutter kept hitting the boulder. People would pass by and laugh at him for persisting when it was obvious that his actions weren't having an effect on results.

But the stonecutter remained disciplined. He knew that just because he didn't see immediate results from his current actions, it didn't mean he wasn't making progress.

The stonecutter resumed and kept hitting the boulder and at some point – maybe on the 50th or 70th hit – the stone didn't just chip, it literally split in two.

Let me ask you a question. *Was it one single hit that broke the stone open?* Of course not, it was a result of his dedication and discipline. *What area of sales should you be more disciplined?*

What could the lack of discipline be costing you and your leaders?

EARN YOUR PH.D. IN RESULTS

Education can get you a job. Self-education can make you a fortune.
MAMA

In the world of education, a PhD is a degree which signifies that a leader has stepped up and committed themselves to excellence in academics. But, in the world of business, a PhD is "the degree" that a leader has stepped up and committed to excellence in action!

Simply put, a PhD in education is about being school smart. But, a PhD in Results is about being street smart. Think about it. Schools test to determine how smart you are, but the streets test to determine how you are smart! *What streets?* Try Wall Street. Visit Main Street. The streets are watching.

It's not about having to go back to school to get years of education to improve your performance. It's about having to go back inside yourself to raise your standards and step up as a seller and leader.

In summary, a PhD in Results is a mindset that is attainable by all. It's a commitment to excellence, action and superior results. *How can you earn your PhD in Results?*

It's simple. You've got to STEP UP!

THE RESULTS ICEBERG

The difference between a successful person and others is not a lack of strength, not a lack of knowledge, but rather in a lack of will.
VINCE LOMBARDI

Over the last 15 years, I've had the unique opportunity to work with a premier sales training company delivering training and consulting to some of the world's finest sales organizations, such as Google, IBM, NASDAQ, Eli Lilly, Medtronic and UPS, just to name a few.

I've discovered that most individuals and organizations do a good job of recognizing that results can and should be improved. Because of that recognition, they invest in skills training, like probing and objection handling, in an effort to produce superior results.

Some even go a step further and provide strategies for implementing these new skills. That's good, but "not good enough!" **Skills training is important, but by itself, it fails to produce the desired results.** *Why?* Because skills are just one of the requirements for superior results. These organizations have the right intent, but have invested in the wrong content.

Imagine an iceberg. Most individuals and organizations spend the majority of their time and money focused only on the tip of the iceberg – Skills and Strategies. But below the surface are the factors that have the most influence on perform- ance and results – your indi- vidual and organizational DNA for Results.

The Results Iceberg

SKILLS
STRATEGIES

STANDARDS
TALENT
EVALUATIONS
PSYCHOLOGY

Limiting your focus to the factors above the surface limits your results. *Why is that?* It's because performance improvement begins from the bottom up, not the top down. In other words, the poor sales skills are often just the symptom for weak sales results. **The root causes are often the lack of individual and organizational commitment, DNA or mental toughness.**

Is it time to rethink your requirements for training results?

TRADITIONAL TRAINING

If either organizational fit or job fit is unsatisfactory, it is almost impossible to increase performance with training or coaching.
CHUCK RUSSELL
Right Person – Right Job

Through my field research with over 100 companies and 25,000 sales professionals, I've observed the initial results that can be achieved when individuals and organizations improve their sales skills and strategies.

Painfully, I've also observed that even with the best skills training, many individuals and organizations fail to advance these results from good to GREAT. *Why?* It's because they have excluded two key requirements for results: DNA and Reinforcement (Coaching). As the illustration shows, the minimum requirement for maximum results is based on effective sales Skills, DNA and Coaching. These requirements are inextricably linked for superior results.

Requirements for Results

BUSINESS EXCELLENCE

If you want to make small, incremental improvements,
then work on your behavior. If you want to make quantum
leaps in improvement, then work on your paradigms.
STEPHEN COVEY

Every year, Fortune 500 companies spend over a billion dollars on training with a mission to improve performance and results. The supposition underlying most of these investments is that mediocre performance is primarily due to the lack of effective skills (tactics) and strategies (manuevering). Sadly, these factors are the primary cause of lackluster performance. **The root cause is often the lack of self-discipline and self-development.**

The harder (older) model that many individuals and organizations use to improve performance is to invest in skills training, then add strategies, and then leave it to the individuals to hand the "self" portion on their own. In short, 90% of the focus is on Skills, 10% on Strategies and basically 0% on Self (evaluation). This results model uses an "outside-in" approach for improving performance. But, this is ineffective because results begin from the "inside-out", not the "outside-in."

The Results Model

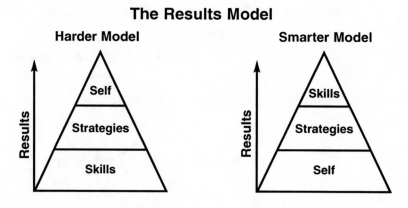

The smarter (newer) model used by top performing individuals and organizations takes the older model and turns it inside out. They begin with the "Self" component – by identifying their DNA for Results and ensuring that it effectively matches the requirements of the job – then they invest in sales training that unleashes their DNA for Results.

Why is this more effective? It's more effective because **"knowledge of self" is the best motivator and behavior modifier in the world!** Furthermore, if a seller lacks the self-discipline or mental horsepower, then even the best skills training in the world can't create improved results. *Does that make sense?* Too often, skills training is an external solution to an inner issue. It's a prescription that treats the symptoms of ineffectiveness, but does not remedy its root causes.

IMPROVE TRAINING R.O.I.

How can you improve the R.O.I. on your training dollars?

Simple, but not easy:

1. Identify your team's personal strengths and struggles – their DNA for Results.

2. Develop and deliver training that is customized to the unique needs of each salesperson.

3. Develop customized performance improvement plans for ongoing reinforcement and results.

Need help? Drop me an email at **daniel@phdinresults.com**

INSIGHTS INTO EXCELLENCE

Success is neither magical nor mysterious. Success is the natural consequence of consistently applying the basic fundamentals.
JIM ROHN

Why do some individuals and organizations fail, while others succeed?

Based on the sales mastery model, here three lists that succinctly answer that question:

SELF	
Top	**Average**
• Raise their bar	• Maintain their standards
• Identify their sales DNA	• Assume they have the talent
• See problems as goals	• See problems
• Plan. Do. Review.	• Guess. Gamble. Mourn.
• Know and do	• Know, but don't do
• Invest in coaching	• Try to go it alone
STRATEGIES	
• Align with Buyer's Psychology	• Lead with Seller's Psychology
• ID client's decision criteria.	• Ignore the client's criteria
• Client-specific strategies	• One strategy fits all
• Competitive Intelligence	• Competitive Assumptions
• Clear value proposition.	• Unclear value proposition
• Remains engaged after the sale	• Walks away after the sale
SKILLS	
• Client-centric	• Seller-centric
• Sell to multiple contacts	• Have one contact
• Pre-call plan	• Plan to wing it
• Link solutions to client's goals	• Feature Dump
• Plan questions	• Plan presentations.
• End call on specific next steps	• End call with general next steps

THE CHALLENGE FROM WITHIN

———·———

The salesperson cried to the universe, "Give me more time." The universe replied, "There is no more time. Give me more of you!"
BILL BAILEY
Author, *Rhythms of Life*

The challenge from within is an internal challenge to consistently step up and give the best that is within you.

Here's a true story as told by Earl Nightingale that illustrates this point:

A former nuclear submarine officer had an interview with the distinguished and formidable Admiral Hyman Rickover, head of the U.S. Submarine Service.

During the interview, the Admiral allowed the young officer to choose any subject he wished to discuss. The young officer carefully chose those subjects that he knew lots about like seamanship, literature, naval tactics, electronics, and gunnery. The Admiral began to ask the young officer a series of questions of increasing difficulty. In each instance, the Admiral proved the young officer knew relatively little about the subject he had chosen.

Then the Admiral looked right into the eyes of the officer and asked, *"How did you stand in your class at the Naval Academy?"* The young officer, who had completed his sophomore year at Georgia Tech before entering Annapolis, had done well and answered with pride, "Sir, I stood 59th in a class of 820!" The young officer sat back to wait for the congratulations. But instead of congratulations, Admiral Rickover asked another question of the young officer, *"Did you do your best?"*

The young officer started to say, "Yes, sir," but regretfully recalled several times at the academy when he could have learned more about the

U.S allies, enemies, weapons, strategy and so forth. Finally, the young officer gulped and said, "No, sir, I didn't always do my best."

The Admiral looked at the young officer for a long time and then turned and asked one final question, which the young officer never forgot or was able to answer. The Admiral asked, "*Why not?*" The young officer sat there for awhile, shaken, and then slowly left the room.

The former submarine officer was Jimmy Carter, former Governor of Georgia and President of the United States.

With regard to that question, *"Are you giving your best?"* *If you could do better, then should you?*

RISE TO THE CHALLENGE

The #1 threat is us. We must not let success breed complacency, cockiness, laziness, indifference or obliviousness to threats posed by the outside world.
HERB KELLEHER
CEO, Southwest Airlines

Here's a summary of the situation:

1. Competition is increasing
2. There's very little that distinguishes one product or service from another
3. Territories are squeezed and more difficult to manage
4. Resources are tighter and you're expected to do more with less
5. Pressure from the CEO to increase sales
6. Pressure from the family to spend more time at home

This is the Results Challenge!

You've got two choices:

1. Step Up

2. Get Stepped On

Some things are beyond your control, but many are not. You have control over your own behavior. You can work smart or you can work hard. You see, **the Results Challenge is really the Challenge from Within.** It's the challenge to raise your standards and STEP UP to next level in business.

1. *What is the #1 area of the STEP UP you want to focus on to get the greatest results?*

2. *What is the #1 action you can take in the next 30 days to improve your results?*

3. *What's the #1 area of improvement for your organization?*

IT'S TIME TO STEP UP!
IF NOT YOU, THEN WHO?
IF NOT NOW, THEN WHEN?

MAMA WAS RIGHT

One day of favor is worth more than a thousand days of labor.
MAMA

The subtitle for this book is How to WIN MORE and *Lose Less* in Business. But sincerely, it could have easily been *Mama was Right*!

In hindsight, I realize I *validated* the Step Up model through my business experiences in sales and leadership. But, I *learned* the Step Up model at home with Mama. She taught me everything that I needed to know to be successful in business and the business of life. *Could the same be said about you and your mom?* I suspect so.

Moms have the unique ability to inspire their children to give their best and aim to become the best. That's *the Magic of Mama.* – Yours and mine. I've dedicated my business, this book and speaking career to my mom. I'd give anything to have another day with her. Unfortunately, I can't have that right now, but you can.

Here's my invitation to you. If your Mom is living, then give her a call right now. Thank her for teaching you how to step up in business and the business of life. And tell her how much you love her.

You know mama was right. *It's time for us to Step Up!*

WHY DO BAD THINGS HAPPEN TO GOOD TRAINING PROGRAMS?

*This Special Report explains
"Why Bad Things Happen to Good Training
Programs" and how to solve this billion dollar
issue. Note: Some elements of this report were
discussed in the previous chapters.*

WHY DO BAD THINGS HAPPEN TO GOOD TRAINING PROGRAMS?

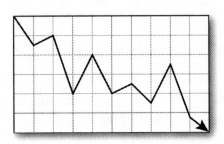

Does this sound familiar?

You just launched a new product or service, but you aren't getting the desired results. Your market share is shrinking and so is your bonus. Your prospects and clients are demanding more value at less cost. You've got a "Results Challenge!" *How are you solving it?*

For many leaders, the solution is to increase revenue by improving sales skills. And training your teams to sell more effectively is a smart start. *So, what's the fatal flaw?* It's to fund the wrong kind of training! Specifically, it's the fatal flaw of investing in a *training event*, rather than a *performance improvement process.*

It typically looks like this; firms pay for the trainer, but don't invest in the follow-up coaching. *What's so bad about that?* Well, it's the coaching that transforms training into results! It's the coaching that develops the new skills and performance.

Here's what a typical training program looks like:

1. The organization identifies a skills deficiency.

2. The organization finds the right training program to improve those skills.

3. The trainer comes in and motivates the team, teaching a set of new skills.

4. The trainer goes away.

5. Those new skills evaporate, along with promised results – back to square one.

6. The CEO and VP of Sales lament *what went wrong and who's to blame?*

What happened? Why do bad things happen to good training programs?

Bad things happen when you only focus on skills. It's ineffective. Skills training is important, but it's only one of the main ingredients in "the recipe for results". By itself, it fails to produce the superior results. *What ingredients are missing?*

As a result of my professional experience and observation inside more than 100 blue-chip companies, I've observed that even with the best skills training many individuals and organizations fail to advance from "good to great" because they are missing Sales DNA and Coaching.

As the following illustration shows, the minimum requirement for maximum results is the combination of the right Sales DNA, plus Skills and Coaching. These are critical ingredients for maximizing the ROI on your training investment. And, without all three ingredients in the mix, you can't create the recipe for superior training results.

Recipes for Results

Let's look at the two Missing Ingredients – the two ways well-intentioned companies set themselves up for failure.

MISSING INGREDIENT #1: SALES DNA

Too often, organizations assume their sellers have the DNA (talent) to perform at a higher level and improve their results. The assumption is that all you need to do is give them even more skills training. This is a "high risk" assumption because if the seller's DNA does not fit the requirements of the job, then training and coaching will yield little improvement.

Think about it. Superior sales results *begin* with a superior match between the requirements of the job and the DNA of the individual. In other words, job fit is job one!

Unless Job Fit is known, the best training anywhere is a hit-or-miss proposition. It can be frustrating for the employee and expensive for the business.
CHUCK RUSSELL
Right Person- Right Job!

A study conducted by *The Harvard Business Review* study determined that in approximately 300,000 cases the only statistically significant difference in job performance and results was "Job Match". Their conclusion:

"It's not experience that counts or college degrees or other accepted factors; success on the job hinges on a fit with the job."

Let's face it, many organizations do a mediocre job of hiring, selecting and matching the talent to the job. And the financial implications are alarming. Consider this daunting data:

- Two of three hires prove to be bad fits within the first year.

– The Harvard Business Review

- Interviews are only 14% accurate in predicting success on the job. The root cause for inaccuracies – personal bias.

  – Michigan State University

- The cost of a hiring mistake is three times the employee's salary.

  – The Gallup Organization

Every year, Fortune 500 companies spend billions of dollars on sales training in a quest to improve performance and results. Those firms assume that the cause of mediocre sales performance is the lack of effective sales skills and/or strategies.

The strategy that many organizations use to improve performance follows a traditional model; I call it the Harder Model. In the Harder Model, the firm begins with skills (tactics), then adds strategies (maneuvers), and then leaves it to the individuals to handle the "self (evaluation)" portion on their own. The "self" portion deals with skills, talents, interests, and personal psychology. The Harder Model creates a house of cards.

In short, approximately 90% of the focus is on Skills, 10% on Strategies and basically 0% on Self. This Model uses an "outside-in" approach to improving performance. It's suboptimal and often "this house of cards falls down and can't get up" because of this truth: **Sales results begin from the "inside-out," not the "outside-in."**

My personal research into the decisions and actions of America's best organizations shows that they follow a Smarter Model (shown below). These organizations take the Harder Model and turn it inside out. They begin with the "Self" component – identifying the employee's DNA and ensuring that it fits with the job demands. Then, they invest in training that is customized to meet the specific needs of that individual sales representative. This Model is your smartest investment for improving sales performance and business results.

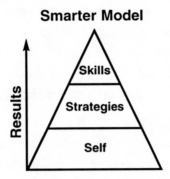

Why is the Smarter Model more effective? It's more effective because **"knowledge of self" is the best motivator and behavior modifier in the world!**

MISSING INGREDIENT #2: COACHING

Our study compared training alone to training combined with coaching. Training alone increased productivity by 22.4%, but training combined with coaching increased productivity by 88%!
PUBLIC PERSONNEL MANAGEMENT

Most organizations do an excellent job of planning for their *training events*, but they neglect to reinforce the learning. The truth is, when you invest in training without reinforcement, you are paying for very expensive entertainment.

The requirements for an excellent skills-training program include three elements:

1. A company commitment to behavioral change

2. An ability to anticipate the discipline dip (the new habits challenge)

3. A coaching plan to build the momentum and help sellers develop new skills

Bottom line: Even great skills training produces weak business results – unless you include the coaching component. In contrast, a mediocre training program can produce better results – if you include the coaching component. Assuming you have hired the right people, **coaching is the single-most important key to improving performance and results.**

Let's further examine this performance improvement process. Once the new skills are understood intellectually, they need to be practiced. The instant you see the seller developing new habits, that's when the coaching program becomes key. Without it, those new habits simply vanish into thin air, along with your training investment.

Whether it's sales, golf, chess or any other skill set, unless your people are helped and guided into applying the new skills consistently, they will likely achieve below-par results. It is the leader's job to hire a trainer who can captivate the audience and effectively teach great skills, but there's more. The leader must find a trainer who can provide one-on-one as well as group coaching.

Again, it is the coaching that ensures your people can actually use the new skills and develop new habits. It is because of the coaching – not just the training – that ensure the results show up on your bottom line.

Reinforcement is the Mother of Achievement

THE STEP UP!

How can you improve the ROI on your training dollars? Follow a simple three-step process. It's simple, but not necessarily easy:

1. Identify your sales team's personal strengths and struggles – their Sales DNA.

2. Deliver sales training that is customized to the unique needs of each salesperson.

3. Develop customized action plans for individual coaching and results.

Now, you have the foundation of a *Performance Improvement Process.* Once implemented, you will begin to produce the behaviors that your CEO expects and Wall Street demands.

IN CONCLUSION

How can you trust that what I've just explained to you is credible?

The truths I've just explained come from my first-hand, professional experience. Yet, more important is *where* I got this experience.

I've worked with a premier sales training company, delivering training and consulting to some of the world's finest sales organizations, inside some of the world's most effective corporations. I've seen over and over again that while the industries are different and the people are different and the products are different – the process for improving results is exactly the same – the union of DNA, skills training and on-going coaching.

I'm not suggesting that a generic approach will work. It probably won't. The training and coaching you pay for absolutely must be customized to your specific industry, products and people. A trainer or coach who is not willing to understand those specifics will ultimately under whelm you.

The good news is, most executives "get it." They understand that results can be improved. And, most of them invest in Sales DNA assessments and Sales Coaching. By meeting the requirements for superior training results, your organization can create, achieve and sustain competitive advantage. You can increase your top-line and bottom-line.

Want to see what it looks like? Want to see how it can work inside your specific organization? Call me personally at 312.315.1591 or **Daniel@phdinresults.com**. I'll show you.

GET YOUR FREE GIFTS NOW!

$99 Value

Log onto **www.stepbook.com** now
before your competition does!

Printed in the United States
90883LV00006B/241-372/A